GOSSIP FROM A MUNIMENT ROOM

BEING PASSAGES IN THE LIVES OF ANNE AND MARY FYTTON
1574 TO 1618

TRANSCRIBED AND EDITED BY
LADY NEWDIGATE-NEWDEGATE

LONDON: DAVID NUTT IN THE STRAND

MDCCCXCVII

Anne and Mary Fytton.
Aged 16 and 18.

Frontispiece.

TO MY HUSBAND

LT.-GENERAL

SIR EDWARD NEWDIGATE-NEWDEGATE, K.C.B.

OF ARBURY

AND

GREAT-GREAT-GREAT-GREAT-GREAT-GRANDSON

OF ANNE FYTTON

LADY NEWDIGATE

INTRODUCTION

THE following passages in the lives of Anne and Mary Fytton have been chiefly gleaned from old letters and papers in the Muniment Room at Arbury.

The task of putting them together in the form of a narrative was undertaken in the first instance for the benefit of the descendants of the elder sister, who have hitherto known little about her. It has since been suggested that so genuine and authentic a record of that distant period may have a wider interest than for family only.

The history of Anne is of necessity a one-sided tale,

being

being drawn from the large correspondence she kept up
with both men and women friends after her marriage,
and though she carefully preserved their letters, her
own, with one or two exceptions, are not at hand to
make the narrative as complete as could be desired.

Mary Fytton, on the other hand, is not unknown to
history, and some interest has been aroused in her of
late years by Mr. Tyler's clever attempt to identify her
with the Dark Ladye of "Shakspeare's Sonnets."*

On one point there is ample evidence. Both sisters
seem to have been unusually gifted with physical and
mental charms, and to have been admired and loved by
persons of note in the era in which they lived.

In order to make this account more complete and
interesting, the letters will not be given in their bald
simplicity, but with explanatory connecting links and
with short biographical and historical facts concerning
the writers.

The letters will follow each other as far as possible in
their proper sequence, but where there are no dates it is
only from internal evidence that they can be placed in
their supposed order.

The

* See Tyler's "Shakspeare's Sonnets." David Nutt, Strand.

Introduction

The spelling is preserved as written, though of the most varied character, even the proper names in signatures and addresses differing as the writer's phonetic sense dictates.

It is unavoidable that occasional references and observations in these letters remain unexplained. As mentioned above, the clue which might be given by the other side of the correspondence is absent. In spite of this drawback, we shall hope to give a fairly consecutive history of some twenty-two years in the lives of our heroines, inventing nothing and withholding neither good nor evil, though the frankness of one or two of the writers is somewhat startling to modern ideas.

CONTENTS

CHAPTER I

Contents

JOHN NEWDEGATE, of Hare- = Amphilis, dau. a[...]eiress of Si[r]
field, co. Middlesex, Esq., | Nevill, Esq., [...] Kt., of co[...]
King's Serjeant 12 Hen. | (2nd son of Sir [...] Dec. 1556.
VIII., d. 16 August 1528, | of Holt, co.
bur. at Harefield. | Rolleston, co. N[...]
 | July 1544, bur. [...]r y, = Sir Richard
 | [...]29, Leveson, Kt.,
John Newdegate, of Hare- = Ann, dau. and h[...]7 of Trentham,
field, Esq., d. 19 June | Hilton, of co. [...]y co. Staffs, and
1545, bur. at Harefield. | Harefield, 9 Ma[...]1. Lilleshall, co.
 | Salop, d. 1559.

John Newdegate, of Harefield, Esq., = Mary, dau.
b. 9 Oct. 1513, M.P. for Middle- | Robert C[...]lter = Anne, dau. of
sex, 1553, 1554, and 1558; m. | of Chesha[...]on, | Sir Andrew
(2) Elizabeth, dau. of Thomas | co. Bucks d. | Corbet, Kt.,
Lovett of Astwell, co. Northants, | (1st wife). | of Moreton
and widow of Anthony Cave, of | | Corbet, co.
Chichley, Esq., bur. at Hare- | | Salop.
field, 20 Aug. 1565. |

 | [...]hard Leveson, Kt.,
 | Admiral, b. circ. 1569,
John Newdegate, of Harefield, Esq., = Martha, da[...]87, Lady Margaret
b. 5 Feb. 1541-2, exchanged | heiress o[...]rd, dau. of Earl of
Harefield for Arbury, co. War- | Cave, Es[...]ngham, d.s.p. 2 Aug.
wick, 20 Nov. 1585; m. (2) circ. | cheley, co[...]
1575-6, Mary Smith, and (3) | 24 Feb. 1[...]
circ. 1577, Winifred Wells, bur. | at Harefiel[...]
26 Feb. 1591-2. | 1575 (1st bapt. at Gawsworth, 24
 | [...]aid of Honour to Queen
 | [...]95. m. (1) circ. 1607,
Sir John Newdigate, Kt., = Anne Fytton, bapt. a[...]heele, Esq., of Perton,
b. 5 March 1570-1, | Gawsworth, 6 October[...] d. 1610; m. (2) John
knighted 23 July 1603, | 1574, m. at Stepney[...] d. circ. 1635. She d.
d. 28 March, and bur. | 30 April 1587, bur. a[...]ed 19 Dec. 1640, proved
at Harefield, 12 April | Harefield, 22 July 1618. Left issue surviving.
1610. |

 | (2nd dau.), b. circ. 1595,
John Newdigate, Esq., | Sir Richard Newdegate, = [...]. 1611-2, Sir Charles
b. 27 May 1600, | 1st Bart., b. 17 Sept. | Kt., of Halsall, co.
Sheriff of Warwick- | 1602, Serj.-at-law and | Their son, Charles
shire, 1626, M.P. for | Judge (of Common- | was created Lord
Liverpool, 1628-9, | wealth), 1654; C.J. | [...]f Brandon and Earl of
m. 1621, Susanna, | 1660, M.P. for Tam- | field, and recovered
dau. of Arnold Luls, | worth, 1660, created | [...]rth estates after long
of London, a Dutch | Bart. 1677; repur- | [...]ith William Fytton of
merchant, d.s.p. surv., | chased Harefield, 1674- | and his son, Sir Alex.
bur. at Harefield, 19 | 75, d. 14 Oct. 1678, | [...]he heirs male.
Nov. 1642. | bur. at Harefield. |

NEWDIGATES O[...]

CHAPTER I

Court & Country Life

NNE and Mary Phyton, Fitton or Fytton were the daughters of Sir Edward Fytton Knight, of Gawsworth in Cheshire, and of Alice, daughter and co-heiress of Sir John Holcroft, of Holcroft in Lancashire. The Fyttons evidently thought much of themselves, and with reason. They were of ancient lineage, had filled posts of honour in the State, and had been knighted for more than one past generation.

Anne, the elder daughter, was born in October 1574, and her only sister Mary some three and a half years later. They had two brothers: the elder, Edward, afterwards a baronet; and the younger, Richard, who died

died unmarried in 1610. Sir Edward, the first baronet, had a daughter, Penelope, who married Sir Charles Gerard. Their son, created Lord Gerard of Brandon, and Earl of Macclesfield, succeeded to the Gawsworth estates on the failure of issue to Penelope Fytton's brother, the second and last baronet.

Anne Fytton, in accordance with the practice of the age, had a husband chosen for her by her parents when she was still a child. At twelve years of age she was married in London to John Newdegate or Newdigate,* aged sixteen, the eldest son of John Newdegate, of Arbury in Warwickshire. The mother of the youthful bridegroom was Martha Cave, daughter and co-heiress of Anthony Cave, of Chichely, Bucks. She died in 1575, a few years after the birth of her son.

Arbury seems to have been securely settled on young John Newdegate. His father married twice after his first wife's death, had several more sons, and accumulated debts to such an extent that he ended his days in the Fleet Prison, dying there at the age of fifty. Nevertheless, he it was who bought Arbury in 1586 from Sir Edmund Anderson, Chief Justice of the Common Pleas in Queen Elizabeth's reign. The present

sent

---

* The name has been spelt in various ways. The present family spell it with an i, excepting the owner of Arbury, who is obliged by will to spell it with an e.

2

sent house had been built a few years previously by
Sir Edmund on the ruins of the old Erdburie Priory.
John Newdegate had to give up his old family manor
of Harefield, in Middlesex, in part payment for Arbury,
retaining only the messuage and farm of Brackenbury,
with the chapel of that name forming the south aisle
in Harefield Church—the burial-place of his family for
many generations. Sir Edmund Anderson soon parted
with Harefield to Sir Thomas Egerton (afterwards
Baron Ellesmere), Lord Keeper to Queen Elizabeth,
who married as his second wife Alice, widow of
Ferdinando, Earl of Derby. The manor of Harefield
was bought back from the heirs of this Lady Derby
by John Newdegate's grandson some ninety years later.
Sir Thomas Egerton and his son, Sir John Egerton
(afterwards Earl of Bridgewater), married, one the
widowed Countess of Derby and the other her second
daughter, Lady Frances Stanley, who is mentioned in
one of the letters that follow.

After the ceremony of marriage between Anne Fytton
and young John Newdigate in 1587, Sir Edward Fytton
seems to have undertaken the young couple's expenses.
Many years later Anne refers to her father's having
kept " her husband, herself, a mayde and two men for
nine years after her marriage of freewill and without
ever haveing paye allowed."

She appears to have been living at home in her father's
house at Gawsworth or in London during this period,

whilst

whilst her boy-husband was probably continuing his education elsewhere.

In a letter from John Newdegate (the spendthrift) "to the Right Worshippfull Sir Edward ffytton Knight," dated November 1588, and entirely on money matters, he adds as a postscript, "Good S^r, let me see my daughter, how I longe to see her."

Anne was at this time just fourteen years old.

The earliest portrait of the two sisters at Arbury must have been taken four years later. It is a double one, three-quarter length, and painted on a panel. Their respective ages of eighteen and fifteen are recorded on the picture. Anne, the elder, has dark hair and eyes and arched eyebrows. She has a gentle, serious expression, and is depicted full face, the shape of an oval contour, whilst her features are small and regular. She is dressed in hoop and ruff in accordance with the costume of the period. Mary's girlish figure is less matured, her complexion fairer and her face narrower with a longer nose. Her lively grey eyes have the alert bright look of her age, indicating, perhaps, already the wit and brilliancy which were among her prominent charms.

It must have been whilst Anne was still an inmate of her old home that she became acquainted with the ill-fated Arabella Stuart, or, as she spells her own name, "Arbella Stewart." The two girls were nearly of an age, Anne being one year the older of the two. She has preserved the following letter from her friend, it

4   being

being as remarkable for the extreme beauty of the writing as for its superiority in diction and spelling to others from persons in the same position of life at that period.

It is addressed "To my good frende, M⁣ʳˢ Anne Newdigate."

I thancke you sweet Mʳˢ Newdigate for your fine cuffes and kinde rememberance of me, hopinge this our acquaintance newlye begonne shall continewe, and growe greater hereafter, Of which I shall be uerye gladde ; as likewise I shall be to see you somtime here when you best can. Thus with my uery hartye comendations to you and my Lady Fitton, I ende. Chessey this 14 of March.

Your assured frende

ARBELLA STEWART.

It was not until 1595 or 1596 that Anne Newdigate finally left her father's house to begin her married life at Arbury. About the same time Mary Fytton received the appointment of Maid of Honour to Queen Elizabeth. Henceforth Anne's and Mary's paths in life took very different directions, but in joy and sorrow, through good report and evil report, in spite of sin and shame, Anne clung to her sister Mary with faithful affection.

One of the earliest letters preserved by the young wife after she left London is from an old friend who much regrets her departure.

To

To my honorable fayre M^ris Ann Newdigate theise at Arbery.

Longeinge so much as I doe to heare of yor good agreement wth the Contrye life I have persuaded my Comforteless Eyes to watch tyll my hand might discover my desire to be satisfied therein. Wright wth every occasion soe shall you hence ordinarily receyve salutacons. Noe Newes heare worthy you, all at this end of the towne are become melancholicque for the want of yor presens. I love you and ever will, and soe I betake you to yor rest, beinge about to take my owne.

Strann this present Mundaye, December 1596.

Yo^rs

HEN CARYE.

We cannot make out for certain who the writer of this letter was.* It could not have been Henry Carey, Lord Hunsdon, the first cousin of Queen Elizabeth, for he died in July of that same year; but it was probably some member of this family, as there are letters of the same period from Lord Hunsdon's daughter Margaret, Lady Hoby, with whom Anne Newdigate seems to have been on intimate terms.

We must now leave Anne to accommodate herself to

" the

---

* There was a Sir Henry Cary who was made Master of the Jewels on June 21, 1603, on James I.'s accession.

6

"the Contrye life" whilst we launch Mary on her career as Maid of Honour to Queen Elizabeth. It was about 1595 that Mary Fytton, being seventeen years old, began her Court life.

Sir Edward Fytton, in his natural anxiety for his young daughter's welfare in her new and trying position, made interest on her behalf with a personage of importance at the Court, who was now Comptroller of the Household, and later on Treasurer.

This was an old friend of his own, Sir William Knollys, son of Sir Francis Knollys, and first cousin once removed to the Queen on her mother's side, through the Careys.

At this time he was upwards of fifty years old, and had been some time married to Dorothy, sister and co-heiress of John, 2nd Lord Braye, and widow of Edmund Brydges, Lord Chandos. She had been left her husband's sole executrix and possessor of much wealth for her life. In his will Lord Chandos grants her this life interest, "as his most faithful and loving wife, for her obedience, truth, and faithful love towards him."

Though Dorothy was a valuable prize as regards her wealth, she must have been considerably older than her second husband, and we have reason to believe he chafed at the chain that prevented his marriage with a younger and fairer spouse.

Sir William's brother, Henry Knollys, had married the only daughter and heiress of Sir Ambrose Cave, a

7   first

first cousin of John Newdigate's mother, Martha Cave. Sir Ambrose was the courtly knight who picked up Queen Elizabeth's garter at a Court Ball, but when he offered it to the Maiden Queen "she would none of it," whereupon he bound it on his left arm and swore to wear it as long as he lived.

We have mentioned this Cave connection with both the Knollys and Newdigates to show that Sir William, who was an old friend of Sir Edward Fytton, had another claim to something more than mere acquaintance with his daughter Anne, through her husband's cousinship with his brother Henry's wife. Mary Fytton being just out of childhood may probably have been a new acquaintance.

The earliest letter we find from Sir William Knollys is addressed :

To my verye lovyng frend Sr Edward Fytton Knight. [How it came into Anne's possession we cannot say.] Sr Edward I am sorye your disease shold so troble you, as yt depryves me off your companye whilst you remayne in London, but I will by no means that you troble yourselff w^{t}h going abroad, but synce you must undertake so great a jornye, be carfful to make yourselff strong until you goe. I wish I wear at libertye to accompanye you to Arbery & so to Drayton.* I will

* His brother Henry Knollys' country place.

I will no ffayle to ffulffill you desyre in playing the
Good Shepperd & will to my power deffend the
innocent lamb ffrom the wolvyshe crueltye & fox-like
subteltye of the tame bests off thys place, wᶜh when
they seme to take bread at a man's hand will byte
beffore they bark, all theyr songs be Syrenlike, and
theyr kisses after Judas ffasshion, but ffrom such
beastes delyver me and my frends. I will wᵗh my
councill advyse your ffayre daughter, wᵗh my true
affection love hyr and wᵗh my sword deffend hyr yff
need be, hir inocency will deserve yt and hyr vertue
will chaleng yt at my hands and I will be as carffull
off hyr weldoing as yff I wear hyr true ffather.
Toching yourselff I will saye onlye this, that your
love to me ys not unrequited & that whensoever eny
occasion shall be offered wherin I maye stand you in
stead I will never ffayle to use my uttermost power.
In the meane tyme wᵗh my best salutations to yourselff and my La : wishing you both health & happines

I remayne ever
Your assured lovyng ffrend
W. KNOLLYS.

Thus Mary Fytton was launched on her Court life
under powerful protection, but the "innocent lamb"
soon turned out to be an arrant coquette, and Sir
William's professions of fatherly affection rapidly grew

warmer,

warmer, and blossomed into ardent love, which he
confides in a series of letters to her sister Anne. Sometimes he veils his sentiments in the language of parable ;
but more often they are expressed in the frankest
terms, apparently with no compunctions in regard to
the existing Lady Knollys.

Mⁿ Newdigate (he writes), your kynd letter to your
deere syster I have seene, wherein I fynd that though
you be nearlye joyned by the law off nature, yeat are
you more surlye united in the bond of love wᶜh
exceedeth all bands and bringeth wᵗh yt in the end a
blessyng where yt ys trulye contynued. Your thanks
I accept as a recompence suffycient ffor my lynes, but
your excuse off not presuming to write agayne I
nothyng allow seming therby to make my white
staff * an argument off your sloth yff I maye so saye,
but to you & yours I desyre neyther to be head nor
ffoote but in that equall proportion where frendshipp
ys like to contynew surest & longest, & what ys
deere to you ys deerest to me. Wherffore once
agayne I will byd you the base hoping you will not
allwayes kepe the gole in sylence. Some reasons
mythinks might breede a better sympathye betwene
us, ffor I ymagyne we both havyng to much Doe
yeat want, though in dyvers respects our suñer ys
turned

* The emblem of his post at Court.

turned to wynter, the one by the ayry element, the other by the earthlye.

The ffayrist fflowers off our gardens be blasted, yours in the budd by some unholsome easterly wynd, myne in the leaffe by the hoare ffrost and the dyfference ys that bycause the wynd maye change your hopes maye revyve & by reason off the contynuall ffrosts my lookyng ffor eny ffrute off my garden ys in vayne, unles the old tree be cut down & a new graff off a good kynd planted.

But I leave to parable and in playne englische wishe you what you most desyre. As ffor me my hopes being desperate & ffortune ever ffrowning, weare yt not that by the sonneshyne off some pleasyng thoughts I wear somwhat relyved I shold dye both in hope & hart. Yeat hope ys the onlye ffoode I lyve by & patience ys my pillow to rest uppon, both wch I wishe you to make your companions as remedyes agaynst all deseases off the mynd. Yf I have benne to long blame the matter wch leadeth me along, yff to bold wth you let my desyre to provoke you to a lyterall quarrell be my excuse, & yff to open empute yt to my trust. But yt ys tyme to leave trobling you eny longer & forgeattyng myselff. Wherffore wishing you all health & hapines both off bodye and mynd I desyre to be estemed in the number off your best ffrends, both ffor the love I beare to youre

father

father & all hys & ffor your owne worthynesse
remaynyng ever this 20ᵗʰ off Maye

> Your assured ffrend
>
> W. KNOLLYS.

It seems difficult to find any excuse for this writer's
open avowal of impatience at the impediments that
obstructed the desired end to his courtship of the
attractive maid of honour. Neither is it easy to understand how Anne, the excellent Anne of whom nothing
but good is known, could by her sympathy permit
these frank avowals of Sir William's love for her sister.
He even seemed so sure of her approval and co-opera-
tion as to ask for her prayers on his behalf in a subsequent letter. Here we find the disadvantage of a
one-sided correspondence. There may have been
extenuating circumstances of which we know nothing.
Otherwise we can only be thankful we no longer live
in the age of "good Queen Bess," but in the more
outwardly decorous days of our Sovereign Lady Queen
Victoria.

The letters which follow are given verbatim, for were
they to be curtailed or any sentences omitted their
historical interest and value would be injured.

They have been considered of sufficient importance to
have been preserved for nearly 300 years in the
Muniment Room at Arbury, though never yet made
known even to the immediate members of the family.

12   It

It is also necessary to remember that letters of this
period were written with infinite pains and much consideration, and consequently have a value far superior
to the hasty scrawls of to-day. From their style and
superscription they appear to have been invariably sent
by hand, and months often intervened between their
dates. We must now let Sir William continue the tale
of his tantalising courtship. In his next letter he refers
to Anne's hopes of becoming a mother, her previous
expectations having been disappointed, as we may gather
from his former remarks.

Honorable La : the more you goe about to disable
your owne worthynes the more doe you make yt shyne
in yourselff & by that means bring me ffarther
endetted to so great a kyndnes. The least good
thought of your well wyshing mynd ys a recompence
suffycient ffor my smale power to afford you what
you are worthye off, but such as they are comand and
think that your Dearest Deare doth not wishe you
better then I doe. As God hath blessed you w'h
encrease, so blessed be you ever & ffreed ffrom all
dyscontents, & though myself can not but be now
uppon the stage & playe hys part who ys cloyed w'h
to much & yeat readye to starve ffor hunger, My
eyes see what I can not attayne to, my eares heare
what I doe scant beleve, & my thoughtes are caryed
w'h contrarye conceipts, My hopes are myxt w'h

dispayre

dispayre & my desyres starved wth expectation, but wear my enjoying assured, I could willinglye endure purgatorye ffor a season to purchase my heaven at the last. But the short warning, the distemperature off my head by reason off the toothake & your systers going to bed w^thout bydding me godnight will joyne in one to be a means that ffor this tyme I will onlye troble you wth these ffew lynes skribled in hast, and wishing you all happynes a good delyverye off your burden, and your syster in the same case justiffyable, I leave you to Gods good protectyon, myself to your dearest systers true love & hyr to a constant resolution to love hym onlye who cannot but ever love hyr best & thus wth my best salutations I will ever remayne

Your most assured ffrend

I would fayne saye brother

W. KNOLLYS.

In the next letter he becomes still more outspoken.

Honorable syster, (I can not cheeose but call you so bycause I desyre nothing more than to have yt so) Your ffayre written letter & more ffayrlye endited I have receaved & read more then once or twyse seekyng to ffynd there wch so much you endevour to put me in hope off. Yt ys true that wynter's cold ys the murtherer off all good ffruts in wch clymat I dwell and doe accompt yt as a purgatorye allotted to me ffor my

manye

manye offences comitted agaynst the Highest, the
rather bycause I am more observant & devoted unto
his creature then to hymselff, from w^{c}h to be delyvered
synce there ys no meanes but the devout prayers &
orasynes off my good ffrends let me entreate your
ffayre selffe to perce the heavens w^h your earnest and
best prayers to the effecter & worker of all things for
my delyverye, & that once I maye be so happye as to
ffeele the pleasyng comffort off a delightfful sumer
w^{c}h I doubt not will yeald me the deserved frute off
my constant desyres w^{c}h as yeat no sooner budd by
the heat off the morning sonne but they are blasted
by an untymelye ffrost, so as in the midst off my
best comfforts I see nothing but dark despayre. I
could complayne off ffortune w^{c}h ledd me blyndlye
into this barren desert where I am readye to starve
ffor want off my desyred ffoode & off myselff that
would suffer my reason to be betrayed by my will
in ffollowyng so blynd a guide. But to all my
wounds I will applye your plaster w^{c}h ys patience, a
vertue I must needs conffesse, but havyng in a sort
lost hyr fforce bycause yt ys fforced. Contynew, I
earnestlye entreate you, your prayer ffor my delyverye, and your best means ffor my obtayning that
w^{t}hout the w^{c}h I am not myselff, havyng allready
gyven my best part to one whose I am more then
myne owne. But I must crye scilence least I speak
to loude, comythyng this secrett onlye to your selff,

to

to whom as I wishe all happynes and your owne
hart's desyre, so will I ever remayne

   Your most affectionat brother

     W. Knowlesse then I would.

Anne's first child, a daughter, was born in 1598. The
godparents or "gossipps" chosen for the baby were
Lady Fytton the grandmother, Anne's greatest friend
Elizabeth Lady Grey, and Sir William Knollys.
Immediately after this happy event Sir Edward Fytton
writes as follows :

Good Nan, God in heaven bless thee and my
daughter,* and contynew thy health and lyfe as my
dearest friend and thereby comfort, next thy poore
mother whose love and kindnes to me and her
chyldren I ffere will shorten her dayes, but shee
shall never waunt that comforte that I canne afforde
her. . . . God blesse yor lytle one and grant thee as
muche comfort I besche him as ever mother had of
child, but I ame sory that yor self will needs nurse
her. . . . Thus longeing soare to see thee . . . faare
well this xvii of May 1598.

    Thy treuest friend

     E^d ffyton.

          And

* Common term for grand-daughter and god-daughter.

And again in another letter dated 3rd of July 1598 :

Nan Newdigate, I ame to think my selfe muche beholdinge to you as a ffather cann be to a daughter. Yo^r mother will needs send ffrelan (?) and I send nobodye but my owne hart w^{c}h ever shalbe w^{t}h you where so ever my bodye is. I will se thee so sone as I canne and y^t is sone as I canne, and untill then I will love thee, and ever remeane mour thine then my owne.

E^D ffYTON.

This latter date may have been that of the Christening, for Lady Fytton writes on the same day :

My good Nan, I pray God bless you and my letle doughter. I longe to hear exceedinglye how you boeth do. I had sent befoer this but that I hoped sume other would have sent that do not. . . . I have sent you a nourse's rewarde x^{ll} to by you a certle for my doughter. I wyll provid sume what when she is beegar to remember mee by. I longe to heer how all thinges abowte your new Charge goeth, for I parswaed myself that my sonne Newdygat wyll not go backe w^{t}h hys worde. I pray God send you well to doe w^{t}h it. And we can do you any good lett us know it and it shalbe don. If you heer any thynge of your sister I pray you let know, for I nevar harde ffrom herr synce. God blese you and

yours

yours and send us all meri to meett. Gawsworth
this third of July.

Your lovyng
mother A. ffYTTON.

Com͂ende mee kyndly to your howsbande.
To my good doughter M͛ꝛ
Anne Newdygat at Erbery.

Anne seems to have been a special favourite with her
great-uncle Francis Fytton, who had married the
widowed Countess of Northumberland.
In a letter from him in this same year he says :

Myne owne good neece, my earneste poore love
unto you makethe me desyros to see you &
especially in yoͬ owne House, and yoͬ kynde
acceptance of my meanynge is soche as it byndethe
me more to you for the same for wᶜh I can but reste
thankefull & so kepe it in my breste. And as my
desyre to knowe of yoͬ abidinge at home or not this
winter was onlye yᵗ I ment to come to see you if
possibly I might . . . but if I possibly maye I
will see you this Christmas if not it shalbe moche
agaynst my good will.

Your Father's house in London this xi of November
1598.

Your owne uncle & affectionat frend to all my powere

FRANCYS FYTON.

I praye

I praye to be remembered to my cosen yo' Husband
and to my younge mistress when she can understand
my langwaige.

To myne especiall good neece M" Newdigate at hir
house at Arbery in Warwyckshyre.

It will be observed that, even so early as this year 1598,
Lady Fytton had cause for anxiety about her daughter
Mary, who seems to have been more confidential with
her sister than with her own mother.

Sir William Knollys accepts the post of "Gossipp" to
Anne's little daughter in the next letter, and at the same
time tenders advice on a subject that is not usually
considered one of the duties of god-parents :

How desyrous I am in person to pfforme the offyce
off a godfather myne owne hart knoweth & you
shold have seene yff I wear w'hin myne owne power,
but such ys my bondage to this place as I have
neyther libertye to please my selff nor satisffye my
good ffrends expectation, amonst wch I must accompt
you in the fformost rank as well ffor your owne
worthynes as ffor being so nerlye united both in
nature & love to those wch I honor much & who
maye more comand me than all the world besyds.
But my thoughts off that partye I will leave to be
discovered not by this base means off penne & paper
but by my selff. Accept I praye you off my lawffull

excuse

excuse ffor not coming my selff, assuryng you that I will be ever readye to pfforme eny frendlye deutye to you; I have entreated my brother Blunt * to supplye my place in makyng your lytle one a Christian soule & gyve yt what name yt shall please you. Imagyne what name I love best and that doe I nominate but reffer the choyse to your selff, and yff I might be as happye to be a ffather as a godffather, I would think myselff exceedyng rich, but that will never be untill one of your owne tribe be a partye player. I shold like nothing that you playe the nurse yff you wear my wyffe. I must conffesse yt argueth great love, but yt breedeth much troble to yourselff & yt would more greave you yff suckyng your owne milke yt should miscarye children being subject to manye casualtyes. But you maye tell me I am more curious in this poynt then I neede but I speak yt in ffrendlye councell not meaning eyther to contrarye your owne will or dysswade you ffrom your resolution yff by a reasonable perswasion your selff think not good to alter your pourpos. Thus w'hout ffarther complements wisshing you a happye mother off manye chyldren & your owne hart's

desyre .

---

* Sir Christopher Blount, third husband of Lettice Knollys. Her first husband was Walter Devereux, Earl of Essex, and her second was Robert Dudley, Earl of Leicester.

desyre wᵗʰ my best salutations I coṁend you to God & will ever remayne

Your assured poore ffrend & gossep

W. Knollys.

To my verye Lovyng ffrend Mⁿ Anne Newdygate.

The suggestion of the writer in regard to the naming of his god-daughter was carried out. She was christened Mary; but Sir William's advice on a more domestic matter was not as effective. Anne was too devoted a mother to abandon any duty towards her child. Henceforth this correspondent always addresses her as his "Gossepp":

Fayre Gossepp the conveniencye of this bearer and the desyre I have not to be behynd wᵗʰ you in eny kyndnes ys cause that I maye not leave you unsaluted. The manye testymonyes you have made off your worthye respect off me bynd me to be thankfull by all the means I maye, and you shall ever be assured I will not ffayle to pfforme the part of a true ffrend whensoever you shall have cause to trye me. I am sorye I can not assure my coṁing to Arberye being under the coṁand off a greater power, but yff it be possible ffor me to break loose but a lytle I will God willing see Drayton and take Arberye in my waye. Untill then I recoṁend you to your best delights & thus wisshing you as much happines as your hart can think wᵗʰ my best salutations to

your

your selff & my blessyng to your lytle one I remayne ever

Your verye assured ffrend
W. Knollys.

Anne Newdigate had other correspondents at this time, one of them being Sir Fulke Greville (or Fowlke Grevyle as he signed his own name), father of the Sir Fulke Greville who afterwards became Lord Brooke.   They were both men of whose friendship she might be justly proud.   Camden says of the elder Sir Fulke, " he was a person no less esteemed for the sweetness of his temper than the dignity of his station. He was a gentleman full of affabilitye, which got the love of the whole countrie.   For in his time no man did bear a greater sway in the countie of Warwicke." In addition to Sir Fulke's other merits he possessed the useful one of always dating his letters, but his handwriting is unusually difficult to decipher, partly owing to old age and partly to the gout, which often attacked his hand and arm.   Occasionally he had to make use of an amanuensis, though always signing for himself.

Anne seems to have been much attached to him, and had given him the title of her " master," presumably from the love and admiration she felt towards him.   The first letter we find from him is written in 1599, when he must have been about seventy-two years old.

Deere esteemed & best beloved servant All ye words in ye world cannot suffycyntly expresse ye Joy &

22   comfort

comfort I take in bearying ye tytle & name off your M^r· Many men are diversely affectted, some take pryde off fayre howses some off theare welth some off fayre wyffs & others off theare chyldrene ; I only glory y^t I have a servant wch conteynes all vertews & ye same draws to her ye trew love & affecktion off all good mynds & myne in good faythe sweete servant in such sort that thoughe I have ye honor to be called your M^r you have ye powre to com̄and me & any thinge I have, & in y^t so redye to obey y^t I shalbe most glad when you shalbe pleased to use y^t y^r awck-tority : My servant farewell, be nott weery in well thinckynge of him whose thoughts ar still bent to do you honor. My syster Grevyle kyndly com̄ends her to you, & yff shee do nott love to speake whatt shee thincks nott (wch I never yett knew her do) then shee loveth you more then exceedyngly. Wee prattle many tymes off you I wyshe your eares glow nott, I desyre to be in all frendly sort remembered to Mr Nudigate, whose felycyty I shall envy ye lesse, yff he wyll accompany you once a year to this howse. My brother salutes you even wth holl hart, I commend my body sole lyff lands & goods into your hands, God prosper you & yours so shall nott I fayle to do well. From Beachampscourt this 20th off August 1599

by him y^t loves & honors you
Your M^r off your own favor & curtesye
ffOWLKE GREVYLE.
The

The next letter, a year later, is written from Coventry, eight miles from Arbury, and is inscribed :

> To my servant best beloved & deerest esteemed never to be changed Mⁿ An. Nudigate geive thes.
>
> My good servant I dare nott lett passe such a messenger wᵗhout my lynes, lest yᵗ may be imputed to me wᶜh I hate above all things, carelessnes or forgetfulnes off so faythfull a servant & so good a frend. I am nott yett so well yᵗ I dare adventure to ryde so farr : Butt when I feele myself able, I wyll vysyte you God wyllinge & in yᵉ meene tyme & ever after love you & be redy to do you pleasure. To yᵉ Lord I leave you & him hartely pray to geive you all things agreable to your noble hart.
>
> From Coventre this 28 off Apreill 1600.
>
>   Your Mʳ & ever assured frend
>   wᵗhout dissimulation
>   ffOWLKE GREVYLE.

There are portraits of Anne and Mary at Arbury which must have been taken about this date. The elder sister, attired in hoop, farthingale, ruff and distended sleeves, has the gentle, serious expression of her earlier portrait. She has the same dark hair and eyes, arched eyebrows and pale complexion. By her side on a table stands her little daughter encircled by the mother's arm. Mary Fytton is in full Court dress with high open ruff, large hoop and puffed sleeves. She must now have

CHAPTER II

Mary's Downfall & Disgrace

E have now reached a period when stirring events took place at Elizabeth's Court in connection with one of our heroines.

Sir William Knollys at this time had other troubles to distract him in addition to his hapless love affair. He writes his next hurried letter when much disturbed by the disgrace of his nephew, the valiant but reckless Earl of Essex: *

Fayre Gossepp, I must crave pardon ffor my so long scilence not growne by a negligent fforgeatfullnes off so good a ffrend, but fforced by a distraction I have

had

* His mother was Lettice, daughter of Sir Francis Knollys.

had concerning the Noble Erle off Essex wᶜʰ hath
made me carles to satisffye myselff or my ffrends.   I
leave to you to ymagyne the discomforts I take heroff
when your syster ys ffayne to blame me ffor my
melancolye & smale respect off hyr who when I am
myselff ys the onlye comffort off my hart. She ys
now well & hath not benne trobled wᵗʰ the mother*
off a long tyme, I would God I might as lawfullye
make hyr a mother as you are, I would be near both
at Arberye to shune the manye greiffs wᶜʰ this place
affordeth & she shold enioye the companye of the
most lovyng & kynd syster that ever I knew. My
hart ys so ffull off sorow at this tyme ffor my lo : off
Essex being dangerouslye syck before hys restraynt as
I am scant myselff. Receave therffore I praye you
these ragged lynes from a broken head as a remembrance off (a) most ffaythffull ffrend who will ever be
readye to doe all good offices wherein I maye stead
you. Thus leavyng ffor this tyme abruptlye wᵗʰ my
best wishes off your best desyres, I comend you to
God & will ever remayne

Your assured lovyng gossepp & ffrend

W. Knollys.

God blesse my ffayre darghter & kisse yt I praye
you kyndlye ffor mee.

No wonder Sir William was thus disturbed about his

nephew

* Fits of hysteria.

27

nephew Essex. He was later one of the four members of the Privy Council sent to parley with him, when Essex, intoxicated by wild ambition, had assembled a crowd of his dependants with every sign of hostile intention at Essex House in the Strand. The other three were the Lord-Keeper Egerton, the Earl of Worcester, and Popham, Lord Chief Justice of England. After some parleying they retired with Essex into the house, when their graceless host bolted the door upon them in the inner apartments, whilst he went off to see what support he might hope for from the City of London. "Thus were these four of the Privy Council confined and left in custody of a rabble, in peril of their lives." In the end they were released by Sir Ferdinando Gorges, and Essex expiated his succession of treasonable attempts with his life.

In the next letter Mary Fytton appears still to be encouraging her elderly lover with hopes that she would be willing to wait for him until he was free to marry her.

Fayre gossepp, your uncles sodayne depture and my comĩng by chance comĩng to London when he was readye to take hys jornye ys cause you must looke ffor no cõpleiments at this tyme, onlye you shall know that true affection ys as well expressed in ffew words as in manye, & I assure my selff your wisdome doth not measure love by lynes. So as havyng

saluted

saluted you wth my best comendacions & assured you
that I will be ever readye to pfforme toward you all
the good offyces off a true ffrend : the best news I
can send you ys that your syster ys in good health &
going to the Court wthin 2 or 3 dayes, though I
think she could be better pleased to be wth hyr best
syster uppon some conditions. Hyr greatest feare ys
that while the grasse groeth the horse maye starve, &
she thinketh a byrd in the bushe ys worth 2 in the
hand. But both she and I must have patience & that
will bring peace at the last. Thus in some hast
wth my best salutations to your selff, and my kyndest
blessyng to my darghter I wishe you your harts
desyre & will remayne ever

Your ffaythffull ffrend and gossepp
W. KNOLLYS.

This is the last letter in which the writer and Mary
seem to have been on the best of terms. A cloud
intervenes which will be explained in due course :

Honorable gossep (writes Sir William), your ffew lynes
but verye pythye and signifficant wear verye welcom
to me & I think I shallbe fforced in as breiff maner
to retorne you myne by reasons off this bearers hastye
depture but wth them a verye thankffull & brother-
lyke acceptance off your kynd remembrance. Yt was
agaynst my will I saw you not this somer I had
pourposed yt but being restrayned off my libertye by

necessarye

necessarye state occasyons I was desposed off other-
wayes. Yt ys true that wynters approch hyndered
my jornye to Arberye and so unhappye I am as I
never ffynd soñer, but being ffayne to ffeede uppon
the dead stork I lyve in doubt ever to enioye the
sweete ffrute off my sommers harvest. My ground
ys covered w⁺h the bramble & the bryer w⁺h untill
yt be grubbed & cut upp ther ys no hope off good.
Yt maye be you contrye wytts maye gyve councell in
such a case. Advyse me I praye you in this extremitye,
and yff I maye once bryng yt to a ffrutffull soyle, I
doubt not but you shallbe ptaker off my longed ffor
husbandrye. This bearer hasteth awaye & I will
ffynd some other tyme to send to you, so as for this
tyme wisshing you your harts desyre I remayne ever

Your most assured ffrend

W. KNOLLYS.

And again :

Fayre Gossepp havyng so convenient a messenger
though my warning be but short I maye not suffer
hym to passe by you w⁺hout some salutations w⁺h in
regard off the humer I am put into though they can
be but melancolye yeat to one to whom I have benne
so much beholdynge as your ffayre selff I will ever be
thankffull & iust. Mythinkes yt ys pytye that 2
bodyes & one mynd so ffirmlye united as your systers
& yours shold not endure so much distance off place,

but

but that you are both bound the one by hyr Maties
servyce the other by a comandyng husband & yeat I
that am at the next dore doe think my selff now
ffarther ffrom the place I most desyre then in the
begynning off my jornye. Such ys the varietye off
this world & the uncertayntye off this tyme I must
lyve in ffrost & snow subiect to blasts & all yll
wynds & shall I ffeare never be so happye as to
possesse the ffayre fflower off the sum̃ers garden. I
hope you dwell under a better clymate where the
sonne somtymes comfforteth though the soyle be
subiect to ffoggs & mists. Make a vertu off
necessytye & synce your lott ffell not to dwell in the
land of promes where all things wear gyven that wear
desyred, work your owne cõtentment out off your
owne worthines & be ever happier then your unffortunate gossepp who will ever be readye to doe you
respectyble servyce remayning ever

Your affectionate ffrend and gossepp
W. KNOLLYS.

Anne's "unfortunate gossepp" seems to have been
when at Court not only figuratively but literally next
door to the abode of the maids of honour.
Sir Nicholas L'Estrange relates the following anec-
dote : "The Lord Knollys" (as he became at James
I.'s coronation) "in Queen Elizabeth's time had its
lodging at Court, where some of the Ladyes and

Maydes

Maydes of Honour us'd to friske and hey about in the
next room, to his extreame disquiete a nights though
he often warned them of it ; at last he getts one to bolt
their own backe doore when they were all in one night
at their revells, stripps off (to) his shirt, and so with a
payre of spectacles on his nose and Aretine in his hand,
comes marching in at a posterne doore of his owne
chamber, reading very gravely, full upon the faces of
them. Now let the reader judge what a sadd spectacle
and pitiful fright these poor creatures endur'd for he
fac'd them and often traverst the roome in this posture
above an hour."

The next events in the Court life of Mary Fytton are
chiefly taken from Mr. Thomas Tyler's work on
Shakspeare's Sonnets,* to whom we are much indebted
for his researches into the history of this Maid of
Honour in order to make good his theory that she was
the Dark Ladye of the Sonnets.

It may be as well to state at once we think this theory
cannot be proved. From the portraits at Arbury,
Mary was in no respect the brunette described by
Shakspeare as follows :

> My mistress' eyes are nothing like the sun,
>   Coral is more red than her lips red :
> If snow be white, why then her breasts are dun ;
>   If hairs be wires, black wires grow on her head ;

I have

* David Nutt, 270 Strand, 1890.

> I have seen roses damask'd red and white,
>> But no such roses see I in her cheeks,

and again :

>> Therefore my mistress' eyes are raven black,
>>> Her eyes so suited, and they mourners seem
>> At such, who not born fair, no beauty lack,
>>> Slandering Creation with a false esteeme.

Mary, on the contrary, was fair, not "dun"-complexioned, her hair was brown, not "black wires," and her eyes were grey, not "raven-black."

Nor have we any hint in the letters that she had any personal acquaintance with Shakspeare.

Certainly, in the year 1600, William Kempe, the Clown in Shakspeare's Company, dedicated his "Nine daies wonder" to "Mistris Anne Fitton Mayde of Honour to most sacred Mayde Royal Queene Elizabeth." The name Anne is plainly a misnomer for Mary, and shows how slight was Kempe's knowledge of the "Mayde of Honour," though doubtless he selected her as his patroness not only on account of her natural gifts, but in order to ingratiate himself with one so high in favour with Queen Elizabeth.

The book gives an account of a journey which Kempe had performed morris-dancing from London to Norwich. In his dedication Kempe says :

> To shew my duety to your honourable selfe, whose
> fauours (among other bountifull friends) make me

33　　　　　　　c　　　　　　　(dispight

(dispight this sad world) judge my hert Corke and my heeles feathers, so that me thinkes I could fly to Rome (at least hop to Rome as the olde Prouverb is) with a Morter on my head. But in a word, your poore seruant offers the truth of his progresse and profit to your honourable view ; receive it I beseache you, such as it is, rude and plaine ; for I know your pure judgment lookes as soone to see beauty in a Blackamoore, or heare smooth speach from a Stammerer, as to finde any thing but blunt mirth in a Morrice dauncer, especially such a one as Will Kemp, that hath spent his life in mad Jigges and merry jestes.

To quote further from Mr. Tyler :

It was in June of this same year (1600) that there was a remarkable festivity at Blackfriars. William Herbert * was present as was also a lady with whom we shall be still further concerned in the sequel. The occasion of this festivity was the marriage of Lord Herbert (son of the Earl of Worcester) with a lady of the Court, M⁵ Anne Russell. The Queen herself was there ; and having come to Blackfriars by water, she was carried from the water side in a lectica borne by six knights. The bride was conducted to church by the nobleman with whom we are now
more

* The W. H. of the Sonnets ?

more particularly concerned, William Herbert (son of Lord Pembroke) and Lord Cobham. The Queen supped and passed the night at Lord Cobham's.

Rowland Whyte, in a letter to Sir Robert Sidney, dated 14th June 1600,[*] says :

There is to be a memorable maske of eight ladies. They have a strange dawnce newly invented : their attire is this : each hath a skirt of cloth of silver, a rich waistcoat wrought with silkes & gold & silver, a mantell of carnacion taffeta cast under the arme, and their hair loose about their shoulders curiously knotted and interlaced. These are the Maskers : My Lady Doritye [Hastings], Mrs Fitton, Mrs Carey, Mrs Onslow, Mrs Southwell, Mrs Bes Russell, Mrs Darcy & my Lady Blanche Somersett. These eight dawnce to the musiq Apollo bringes, & there is a fine speach that makes mention of a ninth, much to her Honor & Praise.

And again, in another letter written shortly afterwards,[†] he says :

After supper the maske came in, as I writ in my last ; and delicate it was to see 8 ladies soe pretily and richly attired. Mrs Fitton leade, & after they had donne all their own ceremonies, these 8 ladys
maskers

[*] "Sidney Papers," ii. 201.   [†] Ibid. 203.

maskers choose 8 ladies more to dawnce the measures. Mⁿ Fitton went to the Queen & woed her to dawnce; her Majestie asked what she was; "Affection," she said. "Affection!" said the Queen, "Affection is false." Yet her Majestie rose and dawnced; soe did my Lady Marques [of Winchester].

In the next January William Herbert became Earl of Pembroke on the death of his father. The goings on at the Court at this time seem to have been notorious:

> One Mⁿ Martin who dwelt at the Chopinge Knife near Ludgate tould me yᵗ she hath seene preists mary gentlewomen at the Courte, in that tyme when that Mⁿ Fytton was in great fauour, and one of her Majestie's maids of honour, and duringe the time yᵗ the Earle of Pembrooke fauord her she would put off her head tire and tucke upp her clothes and take a large white cloake and marche as though she had bene a man to meete the said Earle out of the Courte.*

It must have been about this time that Sir William Knollys writes to Anne in evident distress about Mary's conduct:

> Honorable gossepp so much have I benne ever beholdyng

---

* "State Papers," Dom. Add. vol. xxxiv.; *cf.* "Cal. State Papers," Dom. Add., 1580–1625, p. 411, where the name is erroneously given as "Lytton."

beholdyng to you in your true respectyble good opinion off me as I shold greatlye blame my selff & be thought unworthye yff I shold suffer your letters to returne unanswered, not havyng other means to maniffest how much I accompt my selff endebted to you ffor your many kyndnesses, especiallye in your well wisshing to me in a matter wch most emported me, wch I think will be cleane extinguished though I leave nothing on my part to be donne ffor the contynuaince theroff. But synce I know this discourse will nothing please you, let me assure you that no ffrend you have shallbe more readye to doe all the good offyces of a true ffrend then my selff, wisshing the partye I spoke off beffore so worthye & ffayre a mynd as my gossepp hath. But synce wisshes can not prevayle I will hope the best & praye that God will recteffye yff enything be amisse, accompting my selff the unffortunate man alyke to ffynd that wch I had layed upp in my hart to be my comffort shold become my greatest discomffort. But whye doe I troble you wth these things, let me lyve in your good opinion & I will ever deserve yt, & thus wisshing you all contentment & your harts desyre I will ever remayne

> Your ffaythffull ffrend
> W. KNOLLYS.

Mary Fytton seems to have been launched on a mad

career

career that could only end in disgrace. In a letter of January 26th of this year (1601) from Sir John Stanhope to Sir G. Carew we find this paragraph :

> Of the persecution [which] is like to befall the poor maid's chamber in Court, and of Fytton's afflictions, and lastly her commitment to my Lady Hawkyns, of the discouragement thereby of the rest, though it be now out of your element to think of, yet I doubt not but that some friend doth more particularly advertise you.[*]

Next month, on February 5, in the postscript of a letter written from the Court by Sir Robert Cecil to Sir George Carew, it is recorded :

> We have no news but that there is a misfortune befallen Mistress Fytton, for she is proved with child, and the Earl of Pembroke being examined confesseth a fact but utterly renounceth all marriage. I fear they will both dwell in the Tower awhile, for the Queene hath vowed to send them thither.[†]

Then we come to a letter (in the Record Office) from Tobie Matthew to Dudley Carleton on March 25 which contains the following passage :

> The Earle of Pembroke is committed to the Fleet : his cause is delivered of a boy who is dead.[‡]

Thus

[*] "Cal. State Papers, Carew MSS." 1601–1603, p. 13.
[†] Ibid. p. 20.   [‡] "Cal. State Papers," Dom. 1601–1603.

38

Thus Mary Fytton's short but brilliant career at Court came to an untimely end in dire disgrace. The Maid of Honour especially favoured by the Queen and adored by the Comptroller of the Household only seems to have escaped imprisonment in the Tower by "commitment to my Lady Hawkyns" for her confinement.

It is not surprising that her parents were greatly distressed at this shameful catastrophe, though they still apparently hoped Pembroke could be induced to marry their daughter.

Sir Edward Fytton writes to Anne from London soon afterwards :

> Sweet Nan, I ame very sorrye that you are not well and so is your good Gossepe also [Sir Wm. Knollys?] who hath him comended to you hartylye. I pray you lett heer ffrom you as I doe, I ame in some hope of your Sister's enlargement shortly, but what wilbe the end with the Erle I cannot tell. So sone as [I] canne you shall heere, I have delyverid yo' letter to my Lady Derbye * and so praying you yf this berer cannot otherwayse doe that you help to hyre him a horse to Lycheffild to my owst at the George : and so wth my very harty comendacyons I bid you farrewell this xxijth of Aprill 1601
>
> Y^r loving father & friende
E^D ffYTTON.

* Second wife of Sir John Egerton, the Lord-Keeper.

Good Nan mak sure that this berer have a horse to Lycheffild yf not to Chesshyre.

Her mother adds a few lines on the same sheet :

My owen good Nan this letter must sarve for us boeth. bee waer how you take pheseck. let mee heer how you doo. Whan we heer any good newes you shall heer form mee. God blese you and yours
Your lovyng carfull mother
A. ffYTON.

There is a letter from Sir Edward Fytton to Sir R. Cecil in Lord Salisbury's collection on this matter. It is dated May 16, 1601, and shows that some pressure had been exercised to induce Lord Pembroke to consent to a marriage, but without effect:

I can saye nothinge of the Erle but my daughter is confident in her chance before God and wisthethe my Lo. and she might but meet before in different senes. But for my self I expect no good from hyme that in all this tyme hathe not shewed any kindnes. I count my daughter as good a gentlewoman as my Lo : is though the dignity of honour (be greater onlye in him) w^c^h hathe begiled her I ffeare, except my lo' honesty bee the greater vertuoes.*

This letter is written from Stanner, where Sir Edward was obliged to stop on his road to Cheshire, his daughter
being

* Tyler's "Shakspeare's Sonnets," ed. 1890, p. 90.

being with him and too weak to travel farther. Thus he had obtained her "enlargement" from "my La: Hawkyns" keeping and was carrying her homewards, but apparently in secrecy.

Francis Fytton writes to his great-niece Anne Newdigate eight days later on the 24th of May 1601 :

Myne owne sweete niece I thanke you moche for yo' laste of the 14 of this instante (lately by me received) and so lykewyse for many other before, because I honor you and love you as any the deareste frinds you have. I suppose your father by his stolne jorne into Chesshy(re) (unknowne to me) hathe acquiented you w'h somethinge concernynge yo' Systers estate. Howe true I knowe not for I fynd haltinge w'h me in theyr courses for her. God grante all be for the beste, but for ought I knowe & can see I see nothinge better nor cause of better hope then before & I wisshe all things for her good so well as you desyre w'h is all I can doo, and so good neece fare well ten thousand tymes. ffrom my lodginge the signe of the Black Boye a Chandler's house neare the weste end of the Savoye in the Strand this 24th of Maye 1601.

Your lovinge uncle and assured
poore frind   FRANCYS
fYTON.

I praye you remember me very kindly to your good husband and doo longe to see you boathe.

The

The next letter from Sir William Knollys must have been written after Mary had left the Court and gone to her faithful sister Anne. In spite of all that had occurred the infatuated man seems still a victim to her charms :

> Fayre Gossepp, sweete & pleasant was the blossom off my love, so comffortable & cordiall to my hart as I had therin placed all my delight, I must confesse the harvest was overlong expected yeat had I left nothing undonne in manuryng the same but that yt might have brought fforth both holsom & pleasyng ffrute. But the man off synne [Pembroke ?] havyng in the night sowed tares emongst the good corne both the true husbandman was beguiled and the good ground abused. How much more unhappye am I who though w'h all the care & industrye I can use to bring this soyle to hyr fformer goodnes, yeat ys yt ympossible ffor me to prevayle, & God knows I would reffuse no penance to redeme what ys lost. I write not this to greve hyr whom I have so much loved nor your good selff, ffor ther can be no greater punishment to me then to be a cause off eyther your sadnes to whom I wish so well w'hout comparison. I know your syster ys to apt to be melancolye & you can apprehend hyr greiffs more deeplye then I wish. But you are not alone, neyther can eyther off you be so often remembred w'h sad thoughts as I am ffor that w'h I can not remedye & yeat can never cease to greve

at

at. Be you yeat a comfforter & I will not be wantyng to add enything lying in my power to increase both your contentments, & yff you wear nearer that som-tyme I might playe a part I wold not doubt but to paciffye though not thoroughlye to purge that humer off melancolye. Thus leavyng you both to Gods protection w'h my best salutations & blessyng to my pretye darghter I remayne ever

Your assured ffrend

W. KNOLLYS.

Let me be I praye you kyndlye remembred to M' Newdigate & the more yff he will come dwell at Brokenberyes.*

here are only two more of Sir William's letters to be iven. The next refers to the proposed marriage of his iece Letitia Knollys, daughter and co-heiress of Henry Knollys and Margaret Cave, the latter being first cousin o John Newdigate's mother, Martha Cave :

Fayre gossepp havyng occasion to send this bearer to Drayton I shold ffayle in good manner & might iustlye be accompted ungratfull yff w'h some ffew lynes I dyd not yeald you my best thanks ffor your manye kyndnesses w'h I will ever be readye to requite to the uttermost of my power. Whether yeat you be delyvered or not off your pretye burden I know not,

but

* Brakenbury, John Newdigate's property in Middlesex.

5

but in both I wish you as much joye & comffort as your selff can desyre. I praye you tell Mr Newdigate that hyr Ma^{tye} understandyng off the match betwene Mr Pagett and my neyce doth so well like theroff as she doth not onlye comend hym but all those wch wrought a delyverance off my Neyce ffrom hyr bondage, & y^t wear to long to wryte how exceedinglye she alloweth off the match. But he shall not need to speak to much heroff untill my Nephew Pagett hath benne here & ys desposed to publish yt. Whether your syster be wth you or no I know not, but yff she be add somthyng to your love off hyr ffor my sake who would desyre nothing more off God then that she wear as capable off my love as I have ever meant yt, & what will become off yt God onlye knoweth. Let yt suffyce that my ffyrst love shall ever bynd me to love hyr, your selff and all that love hyr, & thus praying God to send you health & happines I remayne ever

      Your trulye affectionate gossepp

           W. KNOLLYS.

Burne my letters yff you please.

We now come to Sir William Knollys' last letter and give it here, although the date is in advance of the period, to which we must return later. It could not have been written until after July 1603, as it is addressed "To my very lovyng ffrend & gossepp my

44   La :

La : Newdigate;" and John Newdigate was not knighted until the above date.

Fayre & worthye Gossepp, your ffather being the messenger I maye not but aunswer both your lynes wth thys symple penne, & your kyndnes wth whatsoever a true honest hart maye afford, desyrous still to cherish all the branches off that roote into the wch my unchangeable love was so ffyrmlye ingraffed. What yt was your selff & the world dyd know, but what yt ys my hart onlye ys sensible off, yeat maye I boldlye saye no earthlye creature ys M^r off my Love, nor ys like to be, as not willing to trust a woman wth that wch was so treulye gyven & so undeservedlye reiected. Where to ffynd yt I know not, unles yt be eyther hydden in my selff or layed upp by some who suffer yt to rust in some out roome off theyr carles thoughts. But wear I not tyed to a white staff in court & had libertye I would like a knight adventurer never rest untill I ffound better entertaynment ffor so good a guest. But what spyritt guids my penne, or whyther doe I wander. You may guesse at my meaning, she ys not ffar ffrom you that maye dissipher thys rydle & I maye boldlye saye that Marye dyd not chewse the better part, yeat lett hyr I praye you know that no man can wish hyr more happines & contentment then I doe wch I will be readye to maniffest uppon eny offered occasion, &

45   though

though hyr comendacons to me in your last letter wear verye ordynarye yeat let me be remembered to you both in the best manner I can as one who can not seperatt hys thoughts ffrom the remembrance off former bands.

No more at thys tyme, but wishing you & my godsonne * health & happines I remayne ever

Your ffaythffull ffrend & gossepp

W. KNOLLYS.

Excuse me I praye you ffor not writyng to your unkynd syster whose so long scilence maketh me think she hath fforgotten me & herselff, I havyng deserved more than a ffew lynes, but I am pleased synce she will have it so.

In spite of this last touching appeal, Mary does not seem to have been inclined to respond to her old friend's protestations of affection.

Consequently, when in 1605 Dorothy Lady Knollys died, and Lord Knollys (as he was created at the coronation of James I.) became released from the ties he had borne so impatiently, it was not Mary Fytton who succeeded to the vacant place.

Two months after Lady Knollys' decease, her husband married Lady Elizabeth Howard, daughter of Thomas Earl of Suffolk, she being nineteen and her bridegroom sixty-one.

We

* Probably Anne's second son, Richard, born in 1602.

We may here briefly relate the remainder of Sir William's history as extracted from Burke's "Extinct and Dormant Peerages of Great Britain," 2nd Edition, 1840:

In 1614 Lord Knollys was appointed Master of the Wards, and within a short time installed Knight of the Garter. In 1616 he was created Viscount Wallingford, and advanced by King Charles I. in 1626 to the Earldom of Banbury. . . . He died in 1632 at the advanced age of eighty-eight. . . . The subsequent history of this peerage is one of the most curious in the whole record of peerage claims. Upon the decease of the Earl of Banbury, the inquisition found that he died without issue, but leaving a widow, Elizabeth, his last wife. His honours were then deemed extinct, and his estates passed to his collateral heirs, excepting such as he had devised to his widow, who remarried Lord Vaux. In a few years this lady produced two sons, born during her marriage with Lord Banbury, her first husband. They had at first been called Vaux, but now she set them up as the sons of the Earl of Banbury, and gave to the eldest the title of that earldom.

Litigation on this point ensued, with varying results for some generations, until 1813, when the claim to the Earldom of Banbury by the then representative of the family was finally rejected.

Thus Dorothy Knollys was avenged.

CHAPTER III

The Leveson Letters

WE here take up the thread of Anne Newdigate's life, which seems to have been chiefly spent at Arbury amid her increasing family.

In 1600 her eldest son was born and named John, the christian-name of the heads of the family for many generations. A second son arrived in 1602 and was christened Richard, probably after his godfather, Sir Richard Leveson of Trentham and Lilleshall, who was an admiral in the reign of Queen Elizabeth.

Sir Richard was related to Anne through the Fyttons. His grandmother, who was a sister of Francis Fytton, Anne's great-uncle, married Sir Richard Leveson. Their

son

son, Sir Walter, was the father of our Sir Richard, who appears to have been born about 1569, and therefore was only five years older than his cousin Anne.

Richard Leveson entered the navy at an early age, and quickly distinguished himself in the various actions of the latter part of Queen Elizabeth's reign. His promotion was rapid. In 1596 he was knighted, and on James I.'s accession to the throne he was appointed lieutenant of the Admiralty of England, or Vice-Admiral of England for life. In the following year he was made Marshal in the embassage for the conclusion of peace between England and Spain.

When under twenty years of age he was married to Margaret, daughter of Lord Howard, afterwards Earl of Effingham. The marriage turned out unfortunately, Margaret's fate being a lunatic asylum.

There is a full-length portrait of Sir Richard in the drawing-room at Arbury. He is in a black dress suit with knee-breeches, carries a sword suspended from his side, and is standing by a table on which is a globe. In person he is tall and thin, with the complexion and eyes that accord with his red beard and moustache.

He was one of Anne Newdigate's correspondents, whose letters she has carefully preserved, and evidently these cousins were much attached to each other. His usual mode of addressing her is as "Sweet wyff," though at the same time he is on the best of terms with her husband, John Newdigate, whom he speaks of as

49　　　　　　　D　　　　　　　"Jake"

"Jake" or "Jak." It seems to have been in accordance with the fantastic fashion of the time to adopt terms of relationship between close friends which did not exist in reality. Anne has kept letters from women friends who address her as Deare Sister or Swete Sister, and were it not that we know she had only one real sister—Mary, the maid of honour—we should imagine she had been one of a large number of Fytton daughters. Among those who wrote to her in these terms are Elizabeth (Nevill) Lady Grey, Mildred (Cooke) Lady Maxey, and Elizabeth (Beaumont) Lady Ashburnham. Sir Richard Leveson's letters are as frank and hearty as a sailor's should be. He never wanders into the language of parable, like Sir William Knollys, nor wastes pens and paper in elaborate compliments, as was too much the habit of the time. He seems to have been generous to a fault, always sending Anne presents and offering her the use of his purse. His letters have the advantage of being dated, with only two exceptions, the earliest of which must have been written before Sir John was knighted, being addressed :

To my Lovinge Cosin Mᵣ Anne Newdigate at Arbury, these with speed :
Deare partner I can wryte you no Nuse from this place because all Occurrants are According to the Time (semi mortua). They have resolved since my cominge up to send me out agayne, Though the

principall

principall hope which drewe the Quene into this Adventure be alredy returned in to Spaygne.

I have delivered all the reasons and Arguments which my Littell experience can afford to disswade them, because I know that this Time of the yeare doth yeld so poore an expectation of proffit uppon that coast as I feare the voyadge will prove both fruitless and unfortunat.

But since the proiect is ther own the wholl course of the Jorney shalbe caried by ther own concells and Instruction from which I will not varye.

To be short I desire that the world should know how much I contest agaynst it, and therfor yf the successe be ill I do entreat my frendes (since I have no parte of the plott) to endevor by preoccupation to free me from the comon censure of men, which for the most parte is full of mallice and detraction.

Yf I could promyse but the least lyberty to myself I would once more come down to Arbery to byd you farwell : or yf you could be so happy as to be eased from the bondage of that pretty Nursery I would entreat you and my cosin Jake to meet me half way at the least. But since I see impossibillities in both I have purposly sent this messenger to kiss yor handes and to let you know that whersoever he be ether at sea or at land you have still power to comand

RICHARD LEVESON.

London the 15th of Janu :

The

The 4ᵗʰ of feb. I am gone. Com̃end my service to yoʳ sister and tell Mʳⁱˢ Waspsnest* yt she bestowe [the rest is torn off].

Sir Fulke Greville writes to Anne about the same date, also complaining of the ties of her nursery and tendering advice on the subject of her maternal duties, which seem to have exercised the minds of more than one of her correspondents. But with Anne devotion to her children was her most prominent characteristic, and she never abandoned any of the rights of a mother towards her infants, as is her proud boast hereafter.

To his much honored best beloved and deerest esteemed servant Mʳˢ An. Nudygate.

My fondlei beloved servant such as you left me styll I am, thoughe lame & uncertein in my lyms yett styll assured & constant in my love & frendship to you sorowynge in nothinge moore for you butt yᵗ you wyll styll contynew a nurse & by yᵗ meanes hold backe from such as much love & desyre your company : Ytt wyll besydes make age grow upon you & I wyshe you alweys greene & floryshinge as you wer when you were in your pryme. My pylgrimage groweth to an end being over almost to a full poynt off yᵉ yeares yᵗ kynge Davyd appoynts for yᵉ yeares off

* Sir Richard's nickname for little Mary Newdigate.

off a man wᶜh is threescore and ten. I wyshe your
yeares may be dubled wᵗh such happynes & contentment off lyffe yᵗ you may be joyfully heare wᵗh your
frends & after have lyffe everlastynge, & in this
godly humor I leave you to his blessed keepynge.
From your chardge att my Lodge this 4ᵗʰ March
1602[3]. Your ever lovynge trew assured frend
& Mʳ

ffOWLKE GREVYLE.

This letter, from the date, was written shortly before the
death of Queen Elizabeth, which event, as we know,
took place on the 24th of March 1603, and caused
much excitement in the country.
Sir Fulke Greville took a decisive step when the tidings
reached Warwick.
Camden tells us, " Upon the news of the death of Queen
Elizabeth, he being at Warwick at the great assize
came down from the bench and with some of his friends
proclaimed King James which the judges of the circuit
refused to doe."
Anne Newdigate, in her anxiety for news at this critical
period, sends a messenger to London to her cousin Sir
Richard Leveson, who writes to her in answer :

The bearer herof cominge to my Chamber befor I was
up would needes have me to wright somthinge, there-
for you are more beholden to his importunity than

to

to my disposition which at this Instant is ether very slepy or exceedinge sullen.

I am the worst Intelligencer in the world, for I never walke out of my way to learne newes, but what I know you shall have. The kynge is now at Newcastle uppon his way towards London, but we do not expect his Arryvall befor the funerall of ou' late Quene which is appoynted to be uppon Thursday in Æster weeke, and about twenty dayes After we do looke for the Coronation. The Councell standeth as it did, but some Addition is resolved which is yet kept seecret : Southampton is at lyberty and promyseth much to himself : Monioye* I hope shalbe sent for and yo' Sister's mistres uppon Sonday last did looke passinge merely [merrily ?]. The Queenes old Maydes (or rather) the old Queene's Maydes (I hope) shalbe entertayned by the newe, in which nomber Nevill † by my consent shall weare the Admirall's flagge and his flagstaffe also.

Thus much for the Court, now to the Cittye.

Our

---

* Lord Montjoye was created Earl of Devonshire 21st July 1603.
† Mrs. Nevill was appointed Maid of Honour in 1601, and seems to have been a young lady of a lively disposition. She was not reappointed by the new queen. The ancient coat-of-arms of the Nevills contained a galley, and was sometimes called Nevill (Admiral), to distinguish it from the other coat-of-arms Nevill or FitzMaldred (of Raby), also used by the family. This may explain Sir Richard's joke about the Admiral's flag and flagstaff.

ur merchantes with on voyce proclayme peace, then
ll I and many other honest fellowes be layed up in
e wardroppe. London streetes shall be hanged with
loth of Gould when the kinge cometh, The Stones
overed with Arras, the Cunditts runne Renissh
yne alredy, And my Lord Mayor uppon his Ass
anketh his brethren in steed of a stand of pykes to
ceave the Kinge. Ether come up now and se this
ravery or close yo' eyes whillest you lyve, for I hope
ou shall never se it agayne, And let Jaks colpitts
[Jack's coalpits] pay for all. Thus (deare partner)
avinge opened my packe it resteth in yo' power to
ake Choyse of the ware, You have it as I paye for
  and yf my stuff prove good sweet partner let me
ave yo' custome.

London the 12th of Ap' 1603

Yos' in all assurednes

RICHARD LEVESON.

iend me to yo' sister yf she be there, to lyttell
psnest, Jacke and my godsonne, it may be I will see
  shortly.

 reference in this letter to "your Sister's mistris" is
culttoexplain,unlessitreferstotheso-called "mother"
he maids of honour at the time Mary was at Court.
n the context one might have thought it referred to
d Montjoye's wife; but at that time he was not law-
y married to Penelope, sister of the Earl of Essex and
wife

wife of Lord Rich. Charles Blount, 8th Baron Montjoye and afterwards Earl of Devonshire, had distinguished himself in the defeat of the Spanish Armada. The one blot on his career was his connection with Lady Rich (the Stella of Sir Philip Sidney), by whom he had several children and whom he married after her divorce in 1605. In a letter from Francis Fytton to his great-niece Anne we find there was some discussion as to whether she and her husband should come to London at this interesting moment. We cannot say if Anne were able to free herself from the " bondage of her pretty nursery " for the occasion, but her husband was knighted at Whitehall in July of this year, 1603.

In a postscript of Francis Fytton's letter he says : " I praye to be remembered very kindly to my neece, yor Sister " ; and on the next page he adds one or two items of gossip he had heard respecting the Queen's movements from one " Mr. Boold . . . as thoughe the Queene hathe had lately some myshapp (w^{c}h is not to be spoken) and doubted could not keepe the tyme apointed for her comynge." Consequently it was uncertain "when would be the tyme of coronacon if the facte be treue." He also mentions a probability of the " nexte terme " being " put off or at leaste not at london by reason of the greate concourse of people, the heate season of the yeare and feare of the sycknes."

Anne supplements this news with some of her own which she has written on the back of the same letter.

M^r

time. The letter is inscribed "to my much honored ladye the ladye Newdigate," and as it is dated the 14th of March must have been written in 1603–4. It runs as follows :

Maddam

Sr Foulke uppō his returne from Warwicke is much trubled with the gout in his hand and elbow, how it will increase or decrease I know not, but wish the best ; his health.

The occurenses above you have (I assure myself) hard of, if not, there are great preparations for the sollem finishinge the cerremonise of the corronatione. As for the feast, the state thinks fit, it should be spared so great and unnessesarye expence, beinge needles.

Fower Earls are to be created, three of them are these, my lord Chaunsler,* my lord Treasurer,† my lord Cicile; ‡ the fowerth I have not heard named ;

Dewks

* Sir Thomas Egerton, Lord Keeper, was created Baron Ellesmere 21st July 1603, and appointed Lord Chancellor three days later ; he was created Viscount Brackley 7th November 1616, and the Earldom which is said to have been promised to him was conferred upon his son, 27th May 1617.

† Sir Thomas Sackville, Lord Buckhurst, was reappointed Lord Treasurer for life 17th April 1603, and created Earl of Dorset 13th March 1603–4.

‡ Sir Robert Cecil was created Baron Cecil of Essendon 13th May 1603, Viscount Cranborne 20th August 1604, and Earl of Salisbury 4th May 1605.

58

I have now nothinge else to say but do entreat you as you love me to cõmand any thinge that is myne about Lillesell as freely as you do at Arbery. But because I have nothinge but wyld Chattell in a parke I may make you large promysse and of them make no dayntye but send to yoᵒ Cosin Williã Meyor at all times that will obeye yoᵒ warrant.

I intend God willinge to come down so soone as I have despatched on littel peece of a Buysines which I do howerly attend, and then you and yoᵒ sister must shortly after prepare to visite my lodge. In the mean and ever

I will rest

faythfully yos:

. RICHARD LEVESON.

Before Sir Richard writes again Anne seems to have had cause to reproach him for negligence in his correspondence with her. The terms " husband " and " wyff " he makes use of read strangely to modern ears, more especially when cordial greetings are sent to the real husband and " our children."

Sweet wyff it is my fashion I must confess and my fault, yf it be a faulte to be less curious with thos I love than with others whom I less respect. If then my love and observance to you hath not bin so often tendered by Letters as my harte could afforde Let my promyse for Amendment and my open confession

of

of my fault finde pardon for th' offence. On parte
of yo' last letter sheweth some distrust in you of yo'
husbandes love, which I should be very sorry for if I
did not knowe that wher perfect love is setled there
of necessity some sparkes of feare and jelousie must
remayne.

But yf ever I be so unfortunat as to geve iust cause
therof, which shall never be without just precedent
motives : It shall not be don by signes & figures but
in that fashion that doth best beseme an open honest
frend.

Till that Time come, which I hope shall never come,
be assured (sweet wyff) that I am and wilbe

    Yo' faythfull frende and lovynge cosin

        RICHARD LEVESON.

I have sent yo' Chayne though I have seen yo' own
handwrytinge agaynst it : But no more of that yf
you love me : I have sent also some garnetts, when
you se the size yf you will send order to me how yo'
stones shalbe sett I will do my best though I am
badd at it and take it for a favour.

This 3ʳᵈ of May 1604

Comend me to my fellow John and all ou' children.

On the 20th of October 1604 he writes :

Sweet wyff yo' salutations sent unto me by Sʳ Walter

Leveson * are as welcome I assure you as they can be to any man Lyvinge and I thanke you very hartely for yor kinde remembrance.   In these infected Times I know that you will wante many thinges which the Contrey will not yeald : And therfor good Nan lay any thinge uppon me that this place and my power can afforde and use no other body but my self.   In the mean and ever I will pray for yor health and good deliverance and so rest

Yo^r lovinge Cosin to his last hower

RICHARD LEVESON.

Again on the 2nd Nov. 1604 :

Sweet Nan I have sente you by this bearer an odd Ruffe of a New fashion when yor Sister lefte it for you and wythall a poore Remnante of my own which I found in the Corner of a Trunke and do now entreat you to accepte in good parte. I longe to heare of yor safte delivery, which God in heaven graunte you.   And whensoever my love or service may stand you in any steed : as I do now beare the Title of yor husband : so let me carry thus much credit with you that I wilbe more at yor Devotion than the best of husbandes are generally to the best reputed wyffes.

And

* Probably his cousin Sir Walter Leveson of Ashmores, whom he mentions in his will. Sir Richard's father, Sir Walter, died in 1602.

And so sweet Nan with my eveninges and morninges
prayer I coīit you to the handes of the Almighty
Yoʳ faythfull lovinge Cosin till death
RICHARD LEVESON.

In this month of November, Anne's second daughter
and fourth child was born and named Lettice.
Two months later Sir Richard corresponds with her on a
matter of some delicacy concerning the expected arrival
of a royal infant, for which a nurse would be required
of rank combined with other essential qualifications.
Anne Newdigate's claims for this post seem to have
been warmly urged by her friends.

Sweet wyff : in this shorte space of my Arrivall in
these partes I understand not so much towchinge
yoʳ Affayres as I desire to know and therfor you must
not looke for such satisfaction from me now as I
hope to send you by my next.
But fallinge aboard some of yoʳ frendes neer Chancery
Lane I have now brought them to be of ouʳ syde
albeit they were strongly agaynst us.   (They do only
take it to be my project and no other pryvat humor.)
And we are all resolved to runne on Course (vizᵗ to
sound the pleasure of the great one how this great
God send him us shalbe disposed) that thereby yo
frendes may spedely resolve for you, ether to enter-
tayne the proiect or to have the honor of refusinge
it : in the meene Time yoʳ own aptnes and sufficiency

63   shalbe

shalbe so infused to the Q: as I dare assure you no
other will leape over yo.ʳ heade :
I mett yesterday with on of the K : phisitions my
familiar frend and thinkinge to extract somethinge
from him, by way of discourse at last he tould me
that ther were divers Gentlewomens names put in to a
Bill for this imployment and that the K : phisitions
were to examine and geve ther opinions of ther aptnes
for that Charge as by tastinge of ther Mylke etc.
This is probable but rather than my wyff shalbe
drawen in by this kinde of election Ile walke on foote
to Arbery to kepe her at home.
To be shorte I will use all my best faculties in hand-
linge of the buysines wherein Ile either Joyne reputa-
tion wyth hope of preferment or Ile do nothinge.
But alredy I can assure you that you have had very
good offices don for you which shalbe continued wyth
my best helpe and so sweet Nan farwell
This 17ᵗʰ   Yosʳ yosʳ
of Jan : 1604 [5]   Richard Leveson.
For want of paper I will wryte nothinge of Mʳ
Marwood but you have bin too lyberall of my purse.
Good Nan send my unckle busines letter away with
speed.

There seems to have been a letter before this next one
which was not sent :

Sweet wyff I wrote on Letter unto you 4 dayes sithence

which

which hath stayed with me for want of a messenger: Since which Time Ned Maynwaringe hath endevored to enforme him self and as I thinke hath wrytten unto you the substance of his Intelligence. I did ever beleve that the old Lady had some pryvat endes: albeit I will still pursue my end: vizt that you may ether have it to some house of yor own with an absolute power or ells sitt still and have the honour of refusinge it. This messenger is in hast therfor I say no more but desire to heare from you spedely so in hast I rest

Yos^r
RICHARD LEVESON.

This 5th of fe: 1604 [5]
Coṁend me I pray you and excuse me to my fellow John that I wryte not unto him.

The project falls through, and Sir Richard writes again on the 21st of Feb. 1604 [5]:

Sweet wyff since the wrytinge of my last it is secretly tould me that a person of good quallety from whos Alliance I have somtimes taken dependency desireth the keepinge of the Child when it is borne (and is like to have it y^t she seeks) and for the avoydinge of all Competencye it is plotted that a woman of some ordinary respect shalbe the Nurse albeit ther be many sutors.

Thus much hath bin pryvatly delivered unto me and by some casuall discourse I have found it to be probable.

65   E   probable.

probable. I dare not name the persons but you may coniecture whom they are. It resteth then for you wysely and spedely to resolve uppon knowledge wherof yor directions shalbe followed. And so with my love and harty wel wyshinge to all at Arbery I rest

Att yor disposition
RICHARD LEVESON.

The Q. is possest with so good an opinion of yor worth and sufficienty as wythin these 4 dayes she tooke occation to speake of you.

And now we come to Sir Richard's last letter on this subject, in which we find that Anne's old friend and gossip had also been interesting himself on her behalf:

Sweet wyff I can say no more unto you than I wrote unto you in my last which I hope is come unto yor handes : only my Ld Knowles hath promysed to wyrite unto you who discerninge the cariage of thinges desisteth now from ou^r former course but continueth still to you passinge well affected. It may therfor please you in yor next to me to bestow a fewe lynes uppon him Acknowledginge some thankes unto his Lo^{sp} and declaringe yor mynd to be as free from entertayninge unworthy conditions as you were apte at first to nouryshe any hope that mought bringe probabillity of Advancement to yor house and posterity which you are able to expresse in better wordes and I

will

will deliver it yf you so thinke good with some
Addition of my own.

And so sweet wyff nothinge doubtinge but yoᵉ Acceptance of my love will equall any my profession and
performance all shalbe as much tendered to you as
can any

    And so I rest

        At yoᵉ comandment

            RICHARD LEVESON.

This 8ᵗʰ of March 1604–5.

Thus ended this matter as far as Anne was concerned.
The expected royal infant, about whom there had been
so much intriguing, made its appearance shortly afterwards, but only lived two years. Little Princess Mary
lies in Westminster Abbey, her small figure represented
in full Court dress reclining on her elbow upon her
altar-tomb.

A few months after the date of the last letter, in the
August of 1605, Sir Richard Leveson died in the thirty-
sixth year of his age.

This sad event seems to have been unexpected. Sir
Fulke Greville (the younger), afterwards Lord Brooke,
writes to Anne for information concerning it as follows :

Maddam, I thanck you verie much for your kynd
visitation when I was in these parts and will be verie
glad by this messinger to understand of your good

                    health

health whom I send to that purpose, and w⁺hall to intreat you to acquaint mee what you heare of the maner of S⁻ Richard Leveson's death, and what report or opinion there is of his wealth, and how hee hath disposed of his estate : and in whom the trust thereof is specially left. This I desire to know for the love and honor I bare him whilst he lived ; And because therein your affection concurred w⁺h myne I must now respect and honor you so much the more : wherof I pray you rest assured. So w⁺h my verie hartie cõmendations to yourself S⁻ John Newdigate and to poore Penelope I rest

Your assured loving frend
ffULKE GREVYLL.

Good Maddam lett mee know what hee hath done for his sister Penelope.

We have a copy of Sir Richard Leveson's will, dated March 1605, made from the register now at Somerset House, from which the following extracts are taken :

In the name of the Almightie and eternall God Amen. I Richard Leveson of Lillieshall in the countye of Salop, knighte, being of pfecte health and memorye thanks be to God and nowe redie addressed to a iourney beyond the Seas in the service of my kinge and countrye, calling to minde the uncertaintie of all earthly things and that we hould and enioye our selves together with all our temporall blessings

but

but as tenaunts at will to our good God that gave
them, and consideringe the troubles that many tymes
doe insue by the indisposition of mens estate I have
theruppon in the tyme of health resolved to settle
such things as I possesse . . . .

He then recites how he had bought up certain in-
cumbrances on his own and his father's estate, and these
he now dedicates for the purpose of carrying out the
objects of a lease made between himself and Sir Edward
Fytton, Sir Robert Harley, and John Tirrische. In
this lease, which was dated two days before his will,
provision was made for raising £10,000 for such
purposes as he now appoints, viz.: Debts to be paid;
£100 a year to Edmund Manwaringe or John Tirrische
as long as the foresaid lease continues:

Which saide some of one hundred poundes yearly
during the continuaunce of the foresaide lease . . . .
shalbe ymployed by them to such uses and purposes
and such pson and psonnes as I shall appoint unto
them by some private instructions from my selfe.
Item I doe give lymitt and appointe one thousand
pounds pcell of the foresaide some unto my wel-
beloved sister Penelope Leveson als Holborne. Item
I doe give and appointe one thousand pounds to be
paide unto Hughe Burnell in trust to the use and
behooffe of such pson and psonnes as the saide Hughe
Burnell standeth bound to pay the same unto by

due

due obligacōn bearinge date this present mounthe (
Marche which saide some of twoe thousand pounde
to my saide syster and to the saide Hughe Burne
I desier may be paid with all convenient speede.

Then follow various legacies of £100 to £300 t
friends, relatives, and servants, &c. &c.   The residu
of his estate he leaves

To such pson * or psonnes to whom I have conveye
my lands nexte and ymediately after my decease b
one paire of Indentures bearing date the three an
twentieth of this instant Marche. . . . . And (
this my last Will and Testament I doe ordain
constitute and make Sʳ Robert Harley, Sʳ Joh
Leveson, John Tirrische and Samuel Bowdler m
executors.   In witness whereof I have hereunt
subscribed my name and putte my scelle the xxvᵗ
daye of March in the third yeare of the reaigne (
our Soveraigne Lord James by the grace of Go
kinge of England France and Ireland and of Sco
land the xxxviijᵗʰ

RICHARD LEVESON.

This will was proved on the 28th August 1605 by S
Robert Harley, and by John Tirrische and Samu
Bowdler on the 6th of December 1605.

* This seems to have been Sir Richard Leveson, son of Sir Joh
Leveson of Haling, or possibly Sir John himself.

70

CHAPTER IV

Widowhood

I T now behoves us to ascertain from the meagre information at hand how Mary Fytton had been conducting herself since her downfall and disgrace.

As far as the evidence of the letters goes she seems to have given no special anxiety to her family or her friends during this period, and to judge by the frequent salutations sent to her by Anne's correspondents, she must have been often at Arbury with her sister.

Good old Sir Fulke Greville, in a letter dated May 1603, sends his "comendations to your good syster." Sir Richard Leveson mentions her more than once in his

letters

letters in the last chapter as likely to be at Arbury. Sir Edward Fytton, writing to his daughter Anne at a date we know by the superscription must be later than July 1603, says:

> Good Nan God blesse you and yo' syster as my owne lyffe, peruse this inclosure and then send itt yo' mother I pray you. . . . Yo' best Gossepp & honorable frend [Lord Knollys?] comendethe me to tell you he wyshethe you bothe as much hartes ease* as to hyme selfe & every day sayethe he shall not be well untill he see you bothe.

This letter is addressed

> To the Right Worshipfull the Lady Newdigatt att her house at Erbury nere Coventry.
> I pray you hand this at the bull in Coventry to be sent wth speede.

Having noted down these facts in favour of Mary Fytton, it is necessary to record that she is credited by Ormerod, author of the " History of Cheshire," with having had two illegitimate children by Sir Richard Leveson, Kt.
The authority for this scandal is " Sir P. L.'s MSS.," Sir P. L. being undoubtedly Sir Peter Leycester. But Ormerod

* The Heartsease or Pansy was the Fytton crest, and much used by the family as an ornament or device.

72

Ormerod is not accurate in his facts concerning Mary Fytton's later history. He gives her Captain Lougher as her first husband and William Polewhele as her second, when the reverse order should have been recorded.

Mr. Tyler tells us in his "Shakespeare's Sonnets" that Lord de Tabley, on the other hand, asserts that his ancestor, Sir Peter Leycester, in his MSS., gives the order of Mary's two husbands in their proper sequence, and that he further describes Mary's two children by Sir Richard Leveson as daughters. In any case this blot upon Sir Richard's memory rests only on the MSS. of Sir Peter Leycester. Whatever Mary Fytton may have been capable of, this particular scandal seems to be quite unsubstantiated, and, it is to be hoped, is untrue.

It should be borne in mind that Sir Richard Leveson died in August 1605. Up to a late date in 1603 there are constant allusions to Mary Fytton as her sister's guest at Arbury, and there is not a hint of any cause for anxiety or distress on her account, as is the case subsequently to 1605.

It hardly seems possible that so frank and genuine a man as Sir Richard Leveson apparently was could have been capable of writing the letters quoted in the last chapter to his cousin Anne Newdigate, addressing her as "Sweet Wyff" whilst carrying on an intrigue with her only sister. Nor is it likely that Anne would have preserved these letters as valued relics under such circumstances.

Again,

Again, the letter from Sir Fulke Greville (the younger), Sir Philip Sidney's friend, would hardly have been couched in the terms in which he writes to Anne for information respecting Sir Richard Leveson's death if there had been any truth in the record of so prolonged an intrigue. In Sir Richard's will, given in the last chapter, there is no mention of Mary Fytton by name, still less of any provision for her or her problematical children, unless she was to be the recipient of the £100 a year to be disposed of by private instructions.

It is to be hoped that Sir Peter Leycester was mistaken, though it must be acknowledged that Mary's after conduct may have given rise to humiliating scandals concerning her, whether true or not.

It seems probable that as long as Sir Edward Fytton lived Mary was outwardly decorous. He was evidently warmly attached to both his daughters, and Anne, at any rate, fully returned his affection. However, Sir Edward died early in 1606, a few months after Sir Richard Leveson, and it will be seen from two letters, written by Lady Fytton later that same year and early in 1607, that her daughter Mary was again in deep disgrace. Before quoting these letters there is one more to be given from good old Sir Fulke Greville, written by an amanuensis a short time before his death, which took place in 1606. Anne Newdigate seems to have had anxieties of her own at this time in regard to her husband's health, as we gather she was kept at home to nurse him.

Even

Sir Fulke died shortly after the date of this letter, aged eighty.

Lady Fytton (herself now a widow) alludes to his death in the letter we next give. It is addressed " to my best and dearest daughter the Ladie Newdygat at Erburie ":

My owen swette Nan I pray God to blese you and all yours. I am sori for the deth of good Sʳ Fowk Grevill your good ffrynd and mynde ; your loss is gret as can be of a ffrynd hee was a veri ould man, it was marvell hee lyved so long, not doubt but your housband and you shall ffynd his sone a veri honorable gentleman and won that wilbee glade of boeth your ffrynshepis. . . . Your brother doeth enter into phesick tomorrow ffor the payne in his nose God send it well Mʳ Neithsmyth doeth dout but cuer hym affoer Cressymas, if please God. I take no joye to heer of your sister nor of that boy. If it hade plesed God whan I did bear her that shee and I hade bine beried it hade saved mee ffrom a great delle of sorow and gryffe, and her ffrom sham and such shame as never hade Chesshyre woman, worse now than ever. Wrytt no mor to mee of her. Thanke my pritti Jacke for his token. I wyll wer it ffor his sack and sende hym another affoer it bee longe. Comend mee to Mall, Deck and lettle prete Letti. God blesse them all. Lett mee bee kyndly remembared to your housband. Prayng God to send

us

us all well to meet I end, and wyll ever remayn to you A kynde mother.

A. ffYTON.

I would wysshe you to send to your sister this inclosed to see. I have left them unsealed you may reed them and scell them. Good Nan faell not. It standeth much.

Poor mother, what must she not have suffered to write as above about her erring daughter ! Stern as she is in the first part, her mother's heart relents in the post-script, whilst Anne, as ever, seems tender and charitable towards this sister's frailty.

Notice should be taken of " the boy " referred to in this letter in connection with Mary's disgrace. In the following year she married a certain William Polwhele, about whom there seem to have been different opinions in the family. She is known to have had a son by him, and possibly this was the boy born before her marriage. This son was living in September 1609, the date of William Polwhele's will, and a daughter was born sub-sequently, who appears to have eventually married John Gatacre, of Gatacre in Shropshire.

Mr. C. G. O. Bridgeman, of the Chancery Bar, in his exhaustive and valuable researches when compiling a catalogue of the Arbury portraits, has ascertained that a Captain Polwhele served with Sir Richard Leveson in one of his expeditions in 1603, Sir Richard commanding

77   the

the *Repulse* and Captain Polwhele the *Lyons Whelpe*. It
is also worthy of note that the manor of Perton, in
Staffordshire, the place where Polwhele and his wife
resided, was the property of Sir Richard. May not a
confusion have arisen from these facts, and was not
Polwhele the one in fault rather than Sir R. Leveson?
Lady Fytton's next letter gives her opinion of her new
son-in-law, and must have been written in 1607, soon
after the date of the marriage.

> My owen swett Nan I pray God to blese you and all
> yours. I wryt to you the last week that Mr Moer
> was a meen ffor the delyverie of your housbande's
> letter to my Lo: Chaunsler who gave it to his
> Secreteri and commandid hym that Chamberlen
> should answer it, wych I did not well lyke. Your
> brother came hether upon Wensday to see mee, and
> was to goe upon ffryday backe. I showed him your
> letter, and caused hym to go to Sr John Edgerton,
> hopyng hie would have doun hym ffavar in this or
> any other. What deck [Dick ?]* haeth wrytten I know
> not, but this hee tould mee was his answer, that S^r
> John Newdygat wer beste to com and answere it
> hymselfe. It should seem sume other had aferme it
> ——hie would not do your brother that kyndnes, as to
> send for the informacion gyven agaynst your housband
> that

---

* Anne's second brother, Richard Fytton.

78

that hie myght see it, but fell into rallyng agaynst
you ffor speckyng agaynst the mareg of your sister to
Powlwhyell—it was oute of your umar and that hie
was worthee her. My ladi ffrancis * saed she was the
vyles woman under the sone. To concleud they did
use deck so unkynly as hie haeth no grat hart
bournyng to go ther synce Cressynmas. I hade the
kyndest messages from them that could bee and that
they would com see mee. But Poullwhyll is a veri
kave [knave ?] and taketh the disgrace of his wyff
and all her ffryndes to make the wordt [world ?]
thynk hym worthey of her and that she dessarved no
bettar. It is longe to wrytt all I knowe, I would
wyshe your housband to com hether. Gyve it owt I
have sent ffor hym. Lett hym not dowt but to ffynde
as good ffryndes as Chambarlyn. I shall have logyng
for hym. Hie shall faer as I doo. Thus prayng
God to defend us ffrom ower enymes and blese us,
I end, remaynyng ever Your poure, kynde, greved

                                        mother A. ffyton.

Pray your housband thynke no unkyndnes I did not
wryt to hym.

If there had not been some previous scandal between
Mary Fytton and Polwhele, why should her mother
                                                    thus

Lady Frances Stanley, daughter of Ferdinando, Earl of Derby,
and wife of Sir John Egerton, afterwards Earl of Bridgewater.

thus rail against the marriage? We infer that Anne too disapproved of her new brother-in-law. Probably it was not an alliance worthy of a Fytton, but under the circumstances one would imagine it ought to have been welcomed, though in silence.

Be that as it may, when once Mary Fytton became Mary Polwhele her family seem to have accepted the situation,* her great-uncle, Francis Fytton, even going so far as to approve of her husband as a nephew. He writes on Feb. 4, 1606–7, to Sir John:

> Good Sir John Newdigate, you are verie moche beholding to my cosen Polwhele for his diligent care and frindley diligens in laboringe aboute your cause conteyned in the Lord Chaunsler's letter to you. . . .

And in his will, dated March 31, 1608, he makes a special bequest of his "usual ridinge sword" to his "nephewe Mr William Pollwheele whoe married with my neice Mistres Marie Fitton," and also bequeathed to him "the best horse," &c. &c., as a "remembrance & token of my love to him and to my said cozen his now wife," &c.

In this same will, in addition to some plate he bequeaths to Anne Newdigate, he makes the following bequest:

> Also I further will and bequeath to her my said neice the Lady Newdegate my bed being a bed of Downe, wch now standeth in my bed chamber at
> London

* See Appendix.

London wth a cannopie of yellow velvett & curtaynes of yellow double Taffitie & a yellow silk quilte to the same bed belonging, beinge such & the same as my selfe did usually use aboute my bed when I did lye & lodge their, beinge now in the house of Mr Thoms Shippe's Chandler neare to the Savoye in the Strand.

Probably this bedstead still exists at Arbury, and possibly the yellow " Taffitie " curtains also. The bed of " Downe " we trust has long been destroyed.

We quoted above a letter from Lady Fytton to her daughter Anne, in which she hoped that on Sir Fulke Greville's death " his sone wilbee glade of boeth your ffrynshepis." This was evidently the case, for Anne's cousin, Philip Mainwaringe, writing to her from the Court in February 1607-8, says :

Yo^r worthy frind S^r ffulke Grivell is ecsiding well whome I ame very much bound unto wch I doe impute to be for yor Ladiship's sake. If it please yo^u Madam when you next ritt to him to imploy me for the delivery of it I shall take it as a favor.

No wonder Philip Mainwaringe valued this privilege so highly. The life of Sir Fulke Greville (afterwards Lord Brooke) is a romance in itself. Camden says of him "he did so entirely devote himself to the study of real Virtue & Honour that the nobleness of his mind far exceeded that of his birth."

81   F   Lord

Lord Brooke never married, though, as Anthony à Wood tells us, " he lived and died a constant courtier of the Ladies."

After his death under tragical circumstances in 1628 (he having been mortally wounded by a servant who considered himself aggrieved), his body was embalmed and laid in the tomb he had had prepared in his lifetime. It is a handsome structure in black and white marble, occupying the whole of an eight-feet square building, said by Dugdale to have been originally intended for a chapter-house adjoining the Lady Chapel of St. Mary's, Warwick. Here, under a high marble canopy, rest the remains of Lord Brooke, whilst round the four sides of the flat tomb may be read the inscription composed by himself :

FULKE GREVILL
Servant to Queene Elizabeth
Concellor to King James
and frend to Sir Philip Sidney
Trophæum Peccati.

We must now return to Mary Fytton, whom we left safely consigned to the keeping of William Polwhele. This marriage only lasted until 1610, when she was left a widow with one son and one daughter.

We are indebted to Mr. Bridgeman's researches for the discovery of William Polwheele's will, dated September 19, 1609, and proved June 23, 1610.

He

He is described as "of Perton, Co. Stafford." His executors are his wife Mary Polwheele, Sir Walter Leveson, Knt., of Ashmores, and Sir Richard Titchborne, Knt., of Titchborne. The contents of the will are a devise of lands to his wife Mary until their son attains the age of twenty-one, then to his son William Polewheele: a devise of the parsonage of Brownsover als Rugby, Co. Warwick, one third to his wife, one third to his son William, and one third "to such child as my wife is now with child of," or failing such child, to his son William. The residuary legatee is his wife Mary.

The child expected at the date of this will was a daughter Mary, who afterwards married John Gatacre of Gatacre. Thus Mary Polwhele found herself again independent, though as a widow with two children.

Her sister Anne also lost her husband in this same year, 1610. Sir John Newdigate died early in the spring after a trying illness. His family at this time consisted of five children: two sons, John and Richard, and three daughters, Mary, Lettice, and Anne. The last was born in 1607.

When Sir John's illness took a serious turn in the latter part of 1609, Lady Newdigate's maternal love and anxiety induced her to frame a petition without loss of time to Lord Salisbury, Master of the Wards. The purport of this letter was to beg for the grant of the wardship of her eldest son Jack, a boy of nine or ten years old.

In

In those days these wardships appear to have been much
sought after by persons even in the higher ranks of
life, owing to the emoluments they carried with them.
Anne therefore had no time to lose if she would keep
the control of her boys' training and property in her
own hands.

We find a draft copy of this petition of hers to the
Master of the Wards, evidently composed by herself.
It is labelled in the handwriting of her second son as
follows :

> My mother's letter to my Lord Salusbury, Master of
> the Wards for my brother's Wardship when my father
> was sicke.

We give the petition in full :

> Right ho^{bl}
>
> Pardon this unmannerly presumption of a most un-
> fortunate woeman though not unknowne and owte of
> memory wth yor Lo^{sp} yet as manie my nearyst frindes
> as my late father, S^r E^d ffytton my brother wth others
> too tediouse to nominate, having received sundery
> favors from yor Lo^{sp} (there meret none, myne much
> lesse ;) yet being assured of yor owne noble hart's
> disposition and worthie compassion of all I am
> thereby incorraged (in this heavie extremitie being
> altogether frendles) to present my owne weaknes in
> all humble petition to yor noble censure. May it

please

please yor honor that these scraling womanish lynes may bringe to yor vewe this my humble sute. It hath pleased God to visit my husband Sr John Newdigate wth sicknes so that the physitions stand in doubte of his recovery or to fall into a deepe melancholy : that you would bee pleased to bestow the wardship of my pore boye upon me, the unfortunate mother of 5 yonge children all nurssed upon my owne brests and nowe in burthen wth the sixt in this uncomfortable tyme. Ou^r estate is smale, for when my father bestoed me in mariage all my husband's lands in Warwick-shire were assured mee in Joynture wch was not above 200^l a yeare. The rest of his Lands lye in Middle-sex caled Brakenbury wch are rayted to the uttermost and are nowe sett for 220^l a yeare, owte of which 40^l a yeare is estated to my second sonne ; the rest longe since convayed towards payment of debts and daughters' portions, having 3 : which cometh to a very great some for so smale an estate wch being separated, I and all my pore chylderen were utterly ruinated. Hoping to receave the wonted favorse yor honorable clemency hath ever given testimonie of to widdowes and infants, And I shall be readie to yeald such gratuities eyther to my cosen phillip Manwaringe, or to some other as yor Lordship shall apoynt : and I and myne bounde whilst wee breath to solicite the Almightie for yor increase of honor to yor owne noble hart's content. Ceasing to hinder

yor

yor better imployed times, doe humbly take my leave
& remain

Yo^r Lordship's well wishing oratour

A. N.

There are two parchments, both dated May 28,
1610, still existing in the Muniment Room at Arbury,
granting Anne's petition as regards the wardship of
her son and of his lands during his minority. Before,
however, this satisfactory result was obtained, Anne
seems to have had misgivings as to the success of her
petition. We also gather it had been surmised that so
comely and attractive a widow would be likely to
marry again, and the mere suggestion of such a possibility seems to have roused Anne's keen indignation.
We find another paper in her own beautiful handwriting, setting forth her doubts and fears, but to
whom it was addressed we cannot tell.

In the meanwhile we should state poor Sir John Newdigate had died, which was doubtless a happy release, if
the only alternative was his falling into "a deepe
melancholy."

Anne's quaint paper runs as follows :

What I have by my Lo : graunteing me the wardshipp if the marriage takeing from me the thirdes
of my joynture being fond to the Kinge's use ; &
onelye one third parte of Brakenburye also fond to
the Kinge ; the other two parts to the Leasies, so

86   that

that I shall fine to the Kinge & paye a yearlye rent
dureing the minoritye of the ward : for the thirdes
of my owne wch is absolutlye convayed me in joynture & shall loose so much out of my owne estate,
wch I thinke was dearelye purchased for me, my
father S^r Ed Fytton giving 120^l to my marriage ;
keepinge my husband myselfe and a mayde & tow
men 9 yeares of free will without ever haveing paye
allowed ; my late uncle Mr Fras. Fytton under-
takeing 900^l debts of my husband's 7 yeares since,
out of his love to me, & payed them receaveing
them againe to his owne purse but as Mr Newd :
coulde convenientlye spare it to repaye him, of
wch debt there is yet 200^l to be payed.

So that I loose my owne third part of Arberye to
purchase a third owte of Brackenberye and must fine
and paye rent for them boeth : and must be at
charges for the findeing of the officises & what
soever belongeth to the wardshipp, to be repaied
when the ward is 21—if please him.

My Lo : honorablye graunted me boeth the wardshipp of the bodye and land, as in my letter was
included as my sute to him. Therefore I wille
holde it if his Los^p take it not from me ; & I
make no doubte but his honor's hart is to honest to
eate his owne worde : without my desert had urged
him thereto.

What my Lo : shall fine me at or taxe me to paye
I will

I will most willingly, but to loose this interest &
right he so Noblye and freelye gave me : I never will
whilest I breath. But to satisfy my Lo : if he be
possected (by villanye of Mallice to me) of my
brutishenesse to those deare Children that I have
borne of my owne bodye and nurssed of my owne
brests (theye never sucke other milke) thearfore I
had neede to geve good example to them least they
take of the mother,

I will enter into bonnds & toll of the worthyest
frends & nearest kindsmen I have shall joine
wth me, that if it shoulde please God to call me, or
that I shoulde be soe accursed a woeman to marrye
againe, that the wholl interest & comodityes boeth
of the warde's marriage & the lease of the land
from the kinge shall goe fullye & whollye first to
the payement of my husbande's debts, his 3
daughters portions & other legacyes wch amount
to but 100' more, & a reasonable portion to be
provided for this child I now goe with al that the
father haeth not left a pennye : these thinges dis-
charged whatsever the remainder is to my boye
Jacke, being the warde. So that if I marye I will
have estate in nothinge but my owne joynture
dureing my lyfe : and if I lyve maister of my selfe
methinges I deserve to be M^{ris} of my owne children
whilest theye be children. This myselfe & friends
wil be bound to performe to any of worthe my Lo :

shall

shall nominate ; but I scorne to be engaged to any base fellowe.

If a stranger had gott his wardship this had bin freelye gone, and then the ward when he had comen to full age shoulde have had al this to have light uppon him, wch summe in al is 3000^l 300^l & this childe I goe with not provided for. Where I havyng it am resolved to keepe them al and of my owne pore estate (else wil it never be raised out of ninscore pound a yeare unlesse he matche fortunatelye above his lineage deserves), & that I have from the kinge to goe yearly to these fornamed uses ; which I thinke shewes a ill nature in me, and little affectionate love to my children ; with a private purpose of my owne comoditye to defraude my children, for whose sakes onlye God spareth me in this world. For though the warde be my oldest sonne & dearest Childe, haveing but one sonne more, yett the rest are al of the same breede, & I thinke there is a conscience theye shoulde have what their father left them ; wch were they not my owne, I being left his executrixe I should to the uttermost of my powers see faithfullye performed.

I shall marr my marriage by this meanes wch it seemes some report I much gape after. But since so manye deuils goe in shapes of men that my iudgement can not knowe the one for the other ; God deliver me for ever being tyed to anye of them ! For if I

looke

looke for an honest man or a true frend, I must saye as one of the Roman Emperores did, I must goe to the graves for them, for theye are al dead & buryed.

Good, brave Anne ! Though her sentences are involved, her meaning is clear as day. Whatever may have been the destination of this paper, and whether it went forward in these exact words or no, she appears to have triumphed in her object.
Her cousin Philip Mainwaringe, who had a post at Court, writes to her on this subject :

Good Madam, I am soery it was my ill fortune to be absent when I should have done you a frindly office, but yor Letter to my Lo : was soe passionate & moveinge as you did not neede any better meanes for the obtayninge yor desyer. Yet in my hearinge (my Lo : speakinge of Sr John's death & yor pittifull Letter) three or four great persons who I named to Mr Whytall* moved my Lo : very ernestly for yor good, who answered he had & would respect you. When Mr Whytall came to take leave wth me he tould me yor La^p had made choyse of me in yor Letter as yor kinsman who (if pleased my Lo :) you desyred should receve the benefit his L^p would

appoynt

* Anne's faithful steward.

appoynt out of it wch kind respect I feare I shall never merritt but will infinitely acknowlege.

My Ladys Grace writ to my Lo : in the behalf of my Lo : Harrington & his Lady for the Wardship ; His answeere was you had a grant of it alredy, & he was assured if her Grace did know the small vallue of it, she would not have writ for it. Therefore since my Lo : is assured of the meanness of it by yor own Letter you may doe me a favor if you please, to seacond that poynt in my behalf when you next write to my Lo : because you have more power over me then you can challenge of a stranger in whom you have no interest. Thus seasinge yor truble I ever rest

to be disposed of by you

PH : MAINWARINGE.

Fro. Court this 26
of March 1609-[10].

CHAPTER V

Friendship

LL we know of Anne Newdigate's life as a widow only proves that she lived, as ever, first and foremost for her children. We also gather she was an excellent woman of business, and was admirably aided by her faithful servants William Henshaw and William Whitall.

Sir John Newdigate showed his implicit confidence in his wife's loyalty and capacity by leaving her the sole executrix of his will. After his death in 1610, when Anne made her own will, it was mainly a copy of her husband's, although as years went by she had occasion to make later additions to it.

In

1614 she entered into an agreement on parchment
th a sculptor, by name William White, to erect a
onument in alabaster to her husband's memory in
arefield Church, where it may be seen to this day.
John kneels on one side of a desk clothed in armour,
dy Newdigate (also kneeling) on the other side,
bited in flowing black robes with a coif and long
il. Below kneel their five children, the two sons
cing one way and the three daughters the other.
here is no record in baptismal or burial registers of
sixth child, although Anne makes so much capital out
its expected advent in her petition for the wardship
her eldest son. Probably it was stillborn at the time
her trouble.

he inscription on the monument is in both Latin and
nglish. We here give the latter version :

> Here Wisdom's Jewell, Knighthood's Flower
> Cropt off in prime and youthful hower
> Religion, meekness, faithfull love
> Which any Hart might inly moove
> These ever liv'd in this Knight's brest
> Dead in his death with him doth rest
> So that the marble selfe doth weep
> To think on that which it doth keep
> > Weep then who ere this Stone doth see
> > Unless more hard than Stone thou bee.

e must now return to the early days of Anne's
idowhood, and having recorded her indignant protest
the possibility of her being "soe accursed a woeman

3   as

as to marry again," it may be interesting to note what temptations she may have had to belie her own words.

We have a large budget of letters to her from a Francis Beaumont, a scholar and a gentleman, afterwards Master of the Charter-house, who was evidently an ardent admirer of hers and at the same time a warm advocate of the suit of another. This other is only known to us as " my cosyn Saunders."

Francis Beaumont was the second son of Nicholas Beaumont, of Cole Orton in Leicestershire, and of Anne, daughter of William Saunders, of Welford in Northamptonshire. His younger brother, Sir Thomas Beaumont (one of King James's numerous knights), married an heiress who brought him Stoughton Grange in Leicestershire. Sir Thomas also had a house at Bedworth in Warwickshire inherited from his father, and Francis Beaumont, who was unmarried, seems to have spent much time at one or other of his brother's houses. Bedworth, now a grimy mining town, is only three miles from Arbury, and well within easy reach for personal intercourse. It is difficult in these days to imagine where a house suitable for people of condition could have been situated.*

Francis

---

* There is an old house still called Saunders' Hall, which is very likely to have come to Sir Thomas Beaumont through his mother, and is the only dwelling at all probable to have been his residence at Bedworth.

94

Friendship

Francis Beaumont's letters are wordy and overflowing with compliments. They are written with great care in a very neat hand, and though he gives us the place whence he writes and the date of the month, he omits the year, so that it is often difficult to arrive at their exact period.

Anne Newdigate seems to have been in great favour with the whole Beaumont family, including the married daughters, one of whom was Lady Ashburnham and another Lady Dixie.

If we take the earliest letters as having been written about the time of Sir John's last illness, the writer must have then been nearly sixty years of age. Anne had evidently a due respect for his judgment, and consulted him when penning her "passionate and movinge" petition to Lord Salisbury, for there is a much reduced copy in his neat handwriting. We are, however, inclined to think she sent the one we gave in the last chapter, evidently her own composition, and labelled as such by her son Richard.

The following letter seems to have been one of the earliest from Francis Beaumont to Lady Newdigate, as he refers in the postscript to an invalid, who was probably her husband :

My best ladie and of all ladies that ever I knew myne onlie best and most noble Ladie, albeit I am at this present imployed in the behalfe of an olde servant of myne to commend a suitt of his unto

my

my Lo. of Southampton : yet not for any busines to any Lord or Ladie, or to all the Lordes or Ladies in the world, shall the least time overpasse mee where-in I may acknowledge the last dutie I owe unto my best and most worthy Ladie.

And now I appeale from all judgements unto the onelie judgement of my thrise-honored Ladie so dis-creete and so wise, whether she would not thinke mee most unthankfull, voide of all gentilitie, admiration and honestie, if for her last letter onely (though never had been precedent cause) I should not acknowledge my selfe most infinitelie bound unto hir for ever. But now I am occasioned for other haste to play Orlando, not Furioso, but di Lasso,* who sometime, when it is thought that he would ende his songe with some grave cadens and verie long note, doeth of a suddaine cut of all with a quaver or crotchet, his brevitie better expressing the patheticall conceite of the dittie than the longest musicall coardes he could devise to set downe. Thus wishing all healthe & happines to my best Ladie and all hers, I humblie take my leave and rest.   Yours
most infinitelie bound and
readie to be commaunded

Bedworthe the viii of July.   FRANCIS BEAUMONT.

If

---

* Orlando di Lasso, the leading composer (next to Palestrina) of the 16th century. He died at Munich 1594.

If Coventree could have affourded either pomgranates or Lemmons I had sent them unto my frend, but what I could get that I send, and my prayers for him to God, and my man to bring me worde how he is. I doubt not but he shall speedelie recover since God doeth make him a Patient under so kinde and wise a Physitian.

From another letter we quote a paragraph, because it refers to Anne's five children under the emblem of a sinkefoy (cinquefoil), an heraldic term for the pansy or heartsease, which was the Fytton crest :

Your faire & worthelie beloued Sinkefoy I most kindely salute, which being like unto a hartes–ease hath three leaves of one sorte and two of another. I pray God from my verie heart, that they may for ever bring ease of hart to that thrise-worthy Roote that bare them.

He is writing from Stoughton, and adds :

My brother, my Sister, my Neece Ashbornham & my Neece Beaumont desire y^t their loue may verie effectuallie be commended unto you.

In the next letter, written from Bedworth, he makes a request to his " Most honorable Ladie and worthy of mee above all Ladies to be honored," with endless apologies for his boldness, until he at length comes to the point.

97   G   My

My suitt (good Madame) is that you wil please to
bestowe upon mee as an insigne of your favoure,
the copies of your two letters unto my Lo: Treasurer
which you read unto mee in your closet. I
protest unto your Ladis^bp by that dutifull love I owe
you (for a better Sainte wil I not sweare by) that I
wil in such sortt use them as you never shall have
cause to reproove mee and as dearly esteeme them as
a most rare juell of gould, etc. etc.

These letters were probably those given in the last
chapter, as Lord Salisbury, Master of the Wards, was
also Lord High Treasurer up to the time of his death
in 1612. Anne has preserved a copy of her discreet
answer :

Sir, I knowe noe faulte in you worthy of condemna-
tion, therfore can not ajudge you. Mine owne
imperfections I confess them manye ; therfore my
worth noe way challenging such admiration. For
the coppye of those letters you desire, I must not
denye them you. Yett I well knowe theye can be of
no use to you : & the not so doine sending of
them wilbe no prejudice,—for althoughe I shewed
them to yor worthye selfe, it was the more to make
him honored that made me so much bounde to him ;
that woulde so Nobly accept the pore weake &
undiserett solicitation of An unfortunate Woeman his
honoreable harte right censured. But how theye

might

might be if publishedd to the worlds eyes I knowe not. Excuse me till I next see you. For as you are pleased to respect me in an higher estimation then I have or can deserve ; yett I hope never to geve just cause to make you repent that you grounded yo͏ͬ good opinion of her that is resolutlye determined to continewe.

Yo͏ͬ faithfull well wisheing frend
lett my love & best thanks I praye you be conveyed to yo͏ͬ al worthiest Brother & his good Lady.

Francis Beaumont, though so near as at Bedworth, sends an answer to this letter a day or two later, beginning, as usual, full of apologies, lest he should offend " my so noble and worthy a Ladie," and going on to say :

Where your Ladishippe writes that I missense your meaning touching the letters you read unto mee, because therein your purpose was but to show mee the honorable disposition of my Lord, I mistake the matter nothing at all. But let my good Ladie remember that I could not have discerned the graunt of that honorable Lord, without seeing y͏ᵉ thriseworthy request of my honorable Ladie, wherein I can commend no less the wisdome and maner in requesting, than your Ladishippe doeth the honoure and bountie in graunting : and therefore give mee leave (I pray you) as much to honoure my deare Ladie for the one

as

as my good Ladie doeth honoure and thankfullie requite hir good Lord for the other. If you thinke that by wringing myne eye on the one syde I make things that be single seeme to be dubble, let mee alone (good Madame) with that which is myne owne, for myne imparcial judgement in this matter doeth direct mee with such a streight line as I knowe I can not be deceived.

In spite of this letter the writer adds as a postscript :

This day I purpose (God willing) to see my good Ladie, and so to take my leave, my brother & my sister determining the week folowing to goe into Lestarshire, and then to give hir the infinite thanks for those honorable courtesies, which never I can deserve nor requite during my life.
Bedworth ye 2 of Februarie.

In the interview thus foreshadowed, Francis Beaumont seems to have obtained the loan of the desired letters, or rather to have copied them from Anne's dictation. In returning them he writes as follows :

My best and of all most worthie to be my best Ladie, I was unquiet within myselfe untill such time as I had perfourmed your commandment and so have now sent you bothe your letters here inclosed. If they appeare not of such puritie and brightnes as they were when you delivered them, you must or blame or pardon the

rustie

rustie treasurie of my memorie from whense nothing is distiled that looseth not some of the luster it had when it was first infused. My ground worke had bene more sure if I durst have presumed to have borowed your copies : but I had no great minde to intreat them because I found in you so little minde to lend them ; yet as they are there is not (in myne opinion) anything amiss. Your owne they be and yours as much as your owne children be yours, in this onely different, that your children were borne of your bodie and these preatie inanimate creatures borne of your brayne : yet not still borne but borne stil to reproove poore mee. I utterlie discleame from any alteration in them, unles in some one or two places, I have added either if or and : which is an addition like unto two little pinnes, prickt into a faire and wel made vellet gowne, the same neither altering fashion nor substance; but yet peradventure making some one or two pleates sit more closelie then they did before. That you so seriouslie and so often repent your sinne in giving me these two jewels (for no lesse doe I estime of them then of pretious jewels) God forgive you this trespass and I doe, wishing you would still loade mee with moe of these sinnes, until I also finde in myself some motion of repentance. You can not bestowe your favoures upon any the best freindes you have that shalbe more kindelie accepted then of mee, and your most loving freind my neece, who being a

great

great collector of monuments wil, I knowe, in hir
booke of recordes reserve a prime station for my
Ladie Nudigate's letters.   And now mee thinkes, I
may claime some indifferent good place (a litle before
behynde the doore) in your frendshippe, by meanes
of this new aliance with us, your la⁵ᴾ being of late
maried into my neeces sisterhoode.* Reprove me no
more (most worthy Ladie) for making your letters
too common : for had they bene the fairest and finest
virgines in the world I could not have kept them
more chastelie than I did.   The first whereof I
protest, from mee was neither seene nor heard of any
creature living : the second indeed I have rehearsed,
and I will tel you upon what first occasion I was
moved.   A knight (not unknowne to you) commended much a great Ladie (preferring hir above all
others) for hir fayre wryting and most excellent
inditing.   When should I have spoken if now I had
bene silent?   I could upon this offer no less than
compare my best Ladie with hir, who I knowe in
these faire graces by many degrees did farre excel hir?
For what should I have done (good Madame)?
Either I must have bene muet and have layed my
finger upon my lippes, or like a naturall foole have
told [counted] twentie for want of other speache, or
else

* The agreement between Lady Ashburnham and Lady Newdigate
to call each other " sister."

102

else have saied that, which I did say, which was as hott
as a burning cole in my mouthe, before I had uttered
it. After this my neece drawing me asyde (for good
women take great pleasure in hearing other good
women commended) intreated me verie earnestlie to
bestowe of hir a coppie of one of your letters. It is
enough (quoth I) that you heare one of them : a
coppie whereof (as much as I love you) rather than
you shall receive from mee, I wil cut out the tongue
wherewith I utter it. What better observation of
dutie towardes my best Ladie than this could I have
used ? But you say I praysed you. Therein I
offended in deed, but the same was in the scant and
not in the exceeding parte. O miserable world,
wherein wel disposed mindes are rebuked for observ-
ing rowles of charitie, and for commending of vertue !
Madame, my resolution is and never shalbe altered
that my harte shall sooner be taught to leave panting
then my tongue braught to leave praising where
respectivelie I binde myselfe in any observant dutie.
And here I could tel you a prettie tale of my cosyn
Saunders, which I wil forbeare until I see you, and yet
this much in the meantime to bring mee in better
remembrance of the rest ; he blames mee more for
penurie than you doe for plentie, saying it is pittie
that so worthy a subject should ever be praysed by
such a barren and worthless tongue as this of
myne. . . .

No pardon I wil crave for the tediousnes of my letter,
for I must have a pardon *ex officio*, because long tales
and long letters belong to a comforter without limitation and most convenient it is I now use myne office
to my dearest Ladie to make hir way seeme shorter,
while shee is travailing thorowe yᵉ wildernes. I pray
God send you all the happines your owne heart can
desire and as much good fortune to yoʳ worthy
children as he can wishe that loves them dearelie. So
I humblie take my leave, etc. etc.

In this letter we find the first mention of "Cosyn
Saunders," whose suit seems to linger on for a year or
more. The only member of the Saunders family who
would have been a likely aspirant to the hand of Anne
at this time is Matthew Saunders, of Shankton in
Leicestershire. He was the grandson of Francis
Saunders, of Welford in Northamptonshire, and a great-
nephew of Francis Beaumont's mother. He had
married Margaret Skipwith, daughter of Henry Skipwith of Keythorp, but was left a widower in 1605 with
five children. He was knighted in 1617, and died
in 1623.

On the back of the last letter given above Anne has
made a rough copy of the answer she sent this correspondent, in which a gleam of humour appears, where
she alludes to that miscalled "barren tongue," if his
speech were anything like as lengthy as his letters :

These manye testimonyes [she writes] of the con-
tineweance of yo' frendlye respecte of me can not be by
me so worthelesslye esteemed as silentlye to receave
them, and neclect A little thanks (thoughe to pore A
requitall for so rich A curtesie) and thereby also heape
uppon myselfe that wch I hate to be burthened with all,
haveing bin ever preciselye carefull rather to cherishe
A good opinion conceaved of me then to give just
cause to extinguishe it, knoweinge it much easiere to
gett a frend then to keepe one. The adventure of
the loosse of anye such in my record registred woulde
be to me most troblesome. How precious the contrarye in my harts thoughts helde I leave to his
judgement, whose barren tongue is seldome spareinge
in discovereing his much more reverent conceate then
deserved of yo' assured well wishing frend.

A. N.

If this is a specimen of Anne's usual style of letters to
her friends, one can only wonder if so involved and
stilted a production found a place of honour in Lady
Ashburnham's " booke of recordes," she being a great
collector of " monuments." We confess we like Anne's
compositions better when they come from her heart, and
are both " passionate and moveing."

The next letter we give from Francis Beaumont omits
both the date and the place whence he wrote :

Most noble and worthy Ladie I sent yesterday unto

you

you a blanke paper that your good La⁕ might conceive thereby that I held my selfe so infinitelie bound
unto you for your most excellent goodnes, as that out
of my little wealthe of wordes I could not by any
meanes offer that dutie for which most deservedlie I
am indebtted unto you during my life.   In which
conceite of myne (if I did amisse for dutifull love is
ever full of fearefull care) your owne preatie stoarie
of the Canopy, and myne of Timantes* for covering
affectiones wᵗʰ curtaines may be my all sufficient
warrant.   Since which time I have read your little
doubtfull mot, and wel understand what you meant
by receaved, but what by deceaved I can not imagine.
Unwarelie I see, I am faulne into a laberinth out of
the which if my deare Ladie doe not direct mee, hee
whome of hir gracious favoure she called hir comforter, was never him selfe in so much neede to be
comforted, I pray God my best Ladie doe not take
my no ill meaning in some evill parte.   For I protest unto yoʳ La⁕ if there were but one droppe of
bloudde in mee (were the same never so neare my
harte) that would procure any undutifull thoughte
against

* Timanthes lived about 400 b.c. He was a Greek painter of
Sicyon. He is known mainly as the painter of the "Sacrifice of
Iphigenia," in which Agamemnon conceals his uncontrollable grief
by covering his head with his mantle.—The Century Cyclopedia
of Names.

against my so excellent & worthy a Ladie, I could never sleepe quietlie before I had let it out, etc. etc.

Then as a postscript :

The ingredience within your litle guilded pill is stil in my taste more bitter than any aloes.

It is a pleasant variation from these complimentary effusions when we come upon a little local news such as follows in another letter :

Your la^{ps} pleasure was that I should wryte unto you the occasion of my brother's so suddaine departure and speedie appearance upon commandment at the Courte. The matter was unknowne unto my brother him selfe and likewise unto Sr H. Hastinges and therefore may be conjectured, but can not truelie be reported by any other. The manner of their sending for was this. A letter was directed unto them bothe from the Counseile sent by a pourseuant, and commanding that they should without delay make their personall appearance at the Courte, there to understand the Kinge's farther pleasure concerning affaires pertaining unto him selfe. Whether the cause doe proceed from some complainte of the Greene chlothe touching provision (about the which this countrie hath bene often and for many yeares grievouslie trobled) or that the king please to imploy them in quenching the wilde combustion, that, flaming out of our two great houses, hath for this two yeares over-

107   heated

heated all Lestarshire (the one of these Gentlemen
being an assured frend to the one house the other a
neare kyndsman unto the other) or whether he meane
to use their service touching this great sale everie
where reported,—the truthe hereof no man knoweth,
and in roving men doe more often misse than hit the
marke. Yet of this I am assuredlie persuaded y' it
can be no matter of dangerous consequence unto them
selves, being bothe as they are of such respective
cariage.

Your honorable and worthy frend S' John Gray*
liveth : at whome though envie daylie barke, yet
I hope, shee shall never have power to drawe one
droppe of bloode from him. The same day I came
from Arberrie he was at the Assizes at Lestar, where
he was merrie and laught as men doe that are not
dead.

Your most honourable and thriseworthy sister as
faire as beautie it selfe, more fine and prettie than
sparke of vellet and as wittie as Pallas, is, (and so I
long wishe shee may be) in verie good healthe.
Worthy shee is to be loved of that worthy Ladie that
loves hir and shee that loves hir, as worthy to be
loved as any Ladie in the world. Of these two
sisters I have vowed never to speake without some of
their

* Sir John Grey, eldest son of Henry, Lord Grey of Groby, died
vitâ patris in October 1611.

their excellent and most worthy embeliments : so I
thinke I doe now, and so wil I ever do hereafter.
As occasion serves yo' La^{sp} shall heare from me
againe, being verie glad that by this opportunitie, a
way is layed open unto mee to doe a dubble dutie
unto my best and most honored Ladie, etc. etc.

The beginning of the last paragraph must, from the con-
ext, refer to Lady Grey, who always addressed Anne as
" Deare Sister " in her letters, and not to Mary Polwhele,
s might naturally be supposed.

Francis Beaumont fulfils his promise of writing again,
nd dates his letter this time from Bosworth (where he
vas a guest of his niece, Lady Dixie) "ye xx of March":

My last letter (most worthy Ladie) engaged mee in a
bond of dutie to write unto you againe, if occasion
were offered to any such purpose. My brother is
now returned from the Courte, but so many thinges
have happened concerning his journey, as may better
serve for halfe a daies talke then to give but pro-
porcionable matter to the contents of an ordinarie
letter, And therefore I holde it best that these
occurrences be not touched until I see my best Ladie,
which should be (God willing) in these holiedaies,
were I sure that my p̄sence might not become more
troblesome then deserving to be welcome unto you.
For I knowe about this time is your great preparation
to offer your best and hyghest saccrifice unto your

best

best and hyghest Lord, wherein many desire rather
privacie then to be conversant with companie : and I
know not whether yor La^{sp} hath invited any frendes
unto whome if my selfe be a stranger, though I be
but one, yet may I be too many by one for such an
appoyntment, having ever hated importunitie and
inhumanitie as the two most extreme enemies unto
civilitie.

Within fower daies after my last letter Sr John Gray
was at Stoughton, where he spake much good of hir
whome I most honour, for what can any man speake
but good of goodnes it selfe ?

Madame if you had been borne but under some
fortunate Planet, it might have made you so wel
beloved as you are, but that had then proceeded but
from blinde fortune : but myne Ephemerides sayeth,
that you were borne under a most blessed Planet,
which makes you rightlie deserve to be loved of many,
and that proceedes onely from vertue. Of this no
more at this time, but never too much at any time.

My brother Thomas Beaumont is sicke, and I feare
with some danger, my nearest kynsman is verie
extreme sicke, one of my dearest frendes hath the
plague in his house, and I am now going to visite
another frend that lyeth in dying. When so many
so neare and deare unto mee are so ill, I knowe and
feele that I my selfe am not well. Pardon this letter,
which is a monster, begotten by haste and brought

110   forthe

Friendship

forthe by greife, yet accompanied with the same
dutiful affection that all the former have bene and
subscribed as all the rest, etc. etc.

My nephew Dixe and my neece commend their best
and most kindelie affected love unto yor good
Ladishippe.

My many greifes (good Madame) doe move mee to
make many suites unto God : in which I forget not
to pray earnestlie for the healthe and happines of you,
and yours, and shall receive no small comforte, if I
know when I come to Bedworthe that you are all
well, and for the same cause especiallie have sent myne
owne man with this letter, that by him I may
understand how you all are in this queasie * and sickly
time.

* Sick with nausea. See Johnson's Dictionary, folio edition.

CHAPTER VI

Courtship

N the ensuing letters "my Cosyn Saunders'" suit is more openly advocated by his near kinsman Francis Beaumont, although the latter would seem to have been an ardent admirer of Anne Newdigate himself.

He writes from Stoughton on the 17th of January (probably about 1611 or 1612) as follows :

Most noble and worthy Ladie, In my so often accesse and many letters unto your Ladishippe if either hereafter or at this time I commit any crime (for much speache is seldome without deserte of reproofe)

I wil

I wil first of all for them all entreate my good Ladie
to pardon myne erroures, For desiring most earnestlie
to have my Ladie Nudigate not onelie my good
Ladie as shee is to all others, but myne onelie best
Ladie above all others, I wil neither spare wordes nor
workes, suite nor service, that may procure mee hir
good opinion.

Ever since I last see your Ladishippe I have bene
with my dying Pelicane* where I have wrought a
miracle in somewhat reviving dead affectiones that
lay buried for yeares seven foote within the earthe
under a dead bodie.† Here I knowe my good Ladie
can not well understand mee before shee see mee,
and when I wryte I love sometime to leave behynde
mee some obscuritie. For as in entertainment it
argueth indiscretion to set all upon the table at the
first course, and not to reserve something for the
second: so in wryting to so wise and excellent a
Ladie as your selfe, hee that leaveth not a handle in
his former letter to take holde of in his next talke
aymeth not right (mee thinkes) as he should at the
marke hee shootes at. I wil set on a little more,
and yet leave sufficient for a second and third course.
I have contended with Mr. Haake in painting
Phœnix and was not much inferior unto him even
in

---

* " My Cosyn Saunders," as explained hereafter.
† May not this refer to Matthew Saunders' first wife, who died in
1605 ?

in the same lineaments that by his running arte he
endevored to expresse hir.   And what if I should
say that I thinke I did somewhat excell him?   For
he wrought but to the eye and I to the soule; he
but painted upon a carde and I imprinted upon a
harte; he set forthe but a dead beautie but I
discovered a living beautie, and therewithall a mynde
replenished with such vertues as can come under no
skilfull hand to be descryved by a pensill.   In this
maner I have spoken of my Phœnix unto my
Pelicane.   Let not (most worthy Ladie) his labour
hereafter become losse, nor his paines repentance;
which must happen if the end hereafter prove as
hapless as the beginning hitherto hath bene hopeless.
Last of all, and then for this time I leave you.
Absolve (most faire and deare Ladie) this letter from
all suspicion of imposture, protesting unto you, that
neither my tongue herein hath spoken nor my hand
hath wrytten any thing, which my harte hath not
ingenuouslie thought before.   And so offering my
service to be disposed by you I rest most readie
at your commandment
FRANCIS BEAUMONT.
Salute I pray you in my name yor Sister whome the
less I knowe and the more frendlie shee accepteth
it, the more am I behoulding unto hir.

This is the first allusion we have to Mary Polwhele,

who

who appears to have been staying with her sister at Arbury,
and was possibly an advocate for a second marriage to
Lady Newdigate, she herself being on the point of making
a fresh choice on her own account.

The next letter is written from what Francis Beaumont
calls "a sicklie bodie," and is therefore doleful in its
tone. He begins

> It is a comforte in great languishment
> To be bemoned with compassion kinde
> And mitigates the anguish of the minde.

Never was any rule so playnlie confirmed by example, as my Ladies most gratious and comfortable
letter hathe approved this saying of the Poet to be
true : wherein I see that noble spirite of hirs
(which is hir second and worthieste selfe) possess-
ing such varietie and copie of wit as can in most
humilitie show greatest. . . .* Whyle in disabling
hir selfe to comforte, shee hath proved unto mee
that shee is the best comforter that ever comforted
mee since I first breathed of aire. . . .

My neare kinsman that I lefte sicke was my cosyn
Saunders in englische, in latine the dying Pelicane.
I could wishe that in stead of this sicknes he had
my Queene's evill, which is no less in her power to
cure then to cause ; for the recoverie of that disease

is

* Torn off by seal.

is but to hang an Angel about the parties necke which must not be fastened with a ribbon, but with my Queenes owne armes, hir fingers being crossed one within another.

If wyshing were not the sustenance of fooles and that men of better wit might not finde some better foode to feede on, I could wyshe and wyshe againe. Discover not my little conception, for if you finde out this riddle, it may be that I shall have The Sphinxes punishment. I rather desire not to be understoode then to be reprehended. My yesterdaies sicknes stirred up all the humours in my bodie, and in my soule affection and honestie have appoynted a duel. Pardon mee now (my best and most excellent Ladie) or never pardon mee, or rather pardon mee now and ever pardon mee ; for this letter standes in neede of a pardon of course, which being wrytten from a sicklie bodie, is like unto a sicke mannes dreame hanging together like lockes of woole upon a company of bramble briers. And so wishing that my best and dearest Ladie may never want such worthy comforte (when shee needes) as shee hath most bountifullie and honorablie bestowed upon my neede, or better wishing that shee may never be grieved, nor never neede any comforte at all, I commit hir unto his tuition, to whome I wil for ever pray for hir most blessed and happie estate. Bedworthe the xxii of marche, etc. etc.

And

And then as a postscript :

> I would your Lad⁶ᴾ did know how sodenlie and
> strangelie I was cured of my fit the last night, which
> was in such sorte as my Ladie never heard the like,
> nor any that dwells betwixt this and Antipodes.

The next letter has no date, but may well have followed
the previous one :

> Most honorable and my ever best Ladie, not anything
> that came into my handes these many yeares was so
> welcome unto mee, as your good Laᵖ last letter.
> For having before more unadvisedlie than wiselie
> haszarded so worthy a Ladies favoure upon a mum
> chaunce, my diseased soule (after I had perceived myne
> erroure) could finde no reast until such time as your
> most comfortable electuarie was received. Many
> occasiones, I know, might have bene taken, which
> without vehement enforcing would of themselves
> have easelie faulne upon a harde construction : and
> then if my Queene had saied, the hares eares be
> hornes, hornes they must have bene : (what soever
> matter they had bene made of) and where had I bene
> placed, but amongst the number of the unfortunate
> beastes, that upon condemnation of life were dis-
> charged ?
> But I see such is yᵗ honorable and courteous disposi-
> tion of myne excellent Ladie as will not suddenlie

take

take exception against him that truelie honores hir, though occasion might seeme to be offered, and such hir most divine sympathising spirite, as can discerne intention, before almost it come into action, which opinion of myne, confirmed by that noble desert of hirs, if the same shall drawe mee into Palomon's* erroure, I will live and dye in heresie, and never revoke by recantation. . . . When you see my Counsailor, your onely sister, commend I pray you unto hir myne affectionate love, but not my quintessentiall, for that is becomme a confined recusant, having disavowed sacrifice unto all living temples, save onelie unto the living temple of the fairest and dearest deserving Cynthia.†
So craving pardon and wishing never to commit offense I rest

Yours most humble
to be commaunded
FRANCIS BEAUMONT.

I have sent unto my prettie Love my best blacke cocke, hatcht in a raven's neast, and desire yor good La^{sp} to speake for mee, y^t I may be hir best love until hir blacke cocke crowe and I wil desire it no longer.

To judge from the message to Mary Polwhele in this letter,

* *See* Dryden's "Palamon and Arcite."
† Another name for Diana, goddess of the moon.

letter, the writer had made considerable advances in his
acquaintance with her, and one is led to believe she
was aiding him with her counsel in the matter of " Cosyn
Saunders' " courtship.

In our next letter Francis Beaumont refers to an oration
he had made before the King eight years previously,
which shows us the date must be at least 1611, if not
later, James I. having come to the throne in 1603.
He writes from Stoughton on the 3rd of August:

My service remembered to my best and most honored
Ladie, I have sent unto yo' good La'* with this letter
the oration that I made unto the King, which cannot
of yo' parte be so frendlie entertained as of myne it
is willinglie offered, being though not the first, yet
the first of my fruites that ever my best Ladie
pleased to commaund. When it was alive and breathed
by my breathe, it revived both fortune and favoure :
fortune by alowance of the King : favoure by
gratefull acceptance of the two noble men who
intreated mee to perfourme that service. But honor
it never had untill this present day. For though
before it was fortuned and favoured, yet was it never
honored, untill it came to be bounded betweene the
honorable and thrise-happie handes of my most noble
Ladie, more worthie to be honored than all the
Ladies in the world. So now yo' La'* having it (as
it were taken up againe out of the ground after eight

119   yeares

yeares buriall) if you shall suffer some skilfull crowner
to revise the members thereof, there may happelie
appeare a broken leg, a broken arme, or a broken
necke, though at the first by advauntage of haste, it
departed the world quietlie with a suspectles sepulture.
My treasurie (good Madame) hath bene unroofte this
twentie yeare, and so lying open upon winde and
weather, whatsoever now comes out of it can not be
otherwise than either mouldie or rustie. Such as it
is, yours now it is, and myne once it was ; you have
commaunded and I have obeyed : and rather would I
in this, or any other thing, loose the opinion of
myne owne wit, than not yeald obedience to hir will,
whome I honor so unfainedlie.

My cosyn Saunders commendes his service unto you,
and tells me oft that I will loose your good favoure
for fault of wryting : but I tell him that I will never
loose it for any such fault, though wel it may be that
I may loose it for fault in writing, my writing many
times wanting wit, but never will to express the
dutie I deservedlie owe to my so worthy and noble a
Ladie. I assuer you and sweare unto you by my
vowed service, that he loves you dearelie, and hath in
him all the symptomes belonging to y^t languishing
disease.

At the same time I was about this letter Sr George
Belgrave comming to us to Stoughton to dinner, told
mee, that my Ladie Gray, your sister, was brought to

bed

bed of a yong Sr John Gray, and reported unto mee withall (which was strange newes to my brother, my sister and to my selfe) that since our last coming out of Warwickshire your la^p hath bene sicke of the mezels. Of your good recoverie I should be verie glad to heare ; the testimonie whereof, if it were confirmed with your owne most worthy hand, would be unto mee a favour of treble value ; which though often I have desired to see for more excellencie therein than you are desirous to heare, yet was I never so desirous as at this present, when it may witness unto mee that my best Ladie is as well as shee was, when I last left hir. I can but pray unto the all Bountifull Lord to send much safetie to you and yours ; unto whose favorable protection committing you I humblie take my leave and rest, etc. etc.

Then follow the inevitable postscripts :

I must entreat your La^p to pardon mee, though the number of my lines doe farre exceed the proporcion I allotted unto them, when I first began to wryte, ffor before I had sealed up this letter my sister Berkley * was come to Stoughton, who hearing that I was wryting unto you, intreated me verie earnestlie to commend hir love unto your kinde acceptance, and to make

---

* His sister Catherine married, 1st, Anthony Biron ; and, 2ndly, Henry Berkeley.

make knowne how glad shee would be of yo' better acquaintance. When she comes into Warwickshire, she sayeth, shee will visite you : and if you come into Lestarshire, shee desires that shee may see you, and that you shalbe a most welcome guest unto hir.

About ten a clocke at the night came in yo' sister Ashbornham, who hearing my La: Nudigate but once named, fell into such a discourse of love & kindenes, of kindenes and love, of courtesie and complement, of thing and thinges, as neither I can expresse nor this paper wel containe. At the last shee concluded that I must needes convey unto you with all titles of amitie a certaine conjuration, which shee sayeth can not be understoode till you two meete together. God help men, when such fayre ladies turne conjurors. I have sent the same unto you.

My nephew of Coleorton,* who promised mee the bucke in myne absence is gone into Lincomshire, where he meanes to tarrie this monthe, or he knowes not how long him selfe. Now am I going to catche him, who is wylder than any bucke in his parke. If I speed (as I hope I shall) I wil then discharge some little parte of the debt I owe unto my best
Ladie,

* Sir Thomas Beaumont of Cole Orton, the head of the family, succeeded on the death of his father, Sir Henry, in 1607. He was created Viscount Beaumont and died in 1625.

Ladie, to whome I am indebtted in all service I can for ever. And so I wishe you good rest, for now it is an hower past midnight bothe by the clocke and starres, and by my narroweyed scribling that write thus away.

As to the nature of the "conjuration" here said to be enclosed from Lady Ashburnham to Lady Newdigate we cannot tell, but it may have had something to do with "Cosyn Saunders'" wooing, as the "collector of monuments" was also an advocate on his behalf.

The following letter is from her, and tells its own tale :

Deare sister

Because pity is thought to be some ease in calamity & y^t I am so well assured of yor love & kinde respect towardes me, as I know you will bemoane me, I must needs send you worde how ill & painfull a Jorney I had after we parted, falling sicke in the midd way & had much adoe to get home, where I take (as I tolde you) small pleasure or contentment in this little solitary prison y^t I live in, but being here out of hope to injoye my frends presence I often please my fancie wth calling y^m to minde amongst the cheifest of whom yor selfe is never forgotten. And now out of mine owne greefes give me leave a little compationately to remember y^t honest kinde gentleman yor faithfull frend, & my kinsman, whose restles minde makes

him

him more unhappy then eyther losse in his estate, or paine of body can doe, because it being y^t more excellent & sensable parte is of so much ye greater force to pplexe him, whilest his desire & affection (wch being satisfied are ye motives to bring him contentment) are in him continually tossed betweene ye rackets of hope & dispaire, who honoreth you so far as to acknowledg you worthy of much greater preferment in mariage then wth him selfe, yet being of councell wth his owne harte, he saith, none can love you more: his worth & meritt is better manifested daylie by him selfe & conceived by yor witty judgment, then can be expressed by me, though I thinke as much good of him as any frend he hath, doth. You need not think I am brybed, because I speake but sparingly of y^t you know to be his due; & yet I will not so far be led wth kinde regarde towardes him, as I forget my firme love to you, whose greatest happines & best content I wish as mine owne, but ye meanes I am not so well able to judge of as yor selfe & therefore will leave him & his future fortunes to yor good respect & consideration, com̄ending my faithfull affection to yor well deserving selfe & so rest

Yo^r ever louing sister

ELIZA : ASHBORNHAM.

To my very worthy and much esteemed sister

Y^e Lady Nudegate   d.d.

We

We now give Francis Beaumont's two last letters, lengthy as they are, because they give us the curious admixture of his own ardent admiration for his "best Ladie" with an equally impassioned advocacy of his "Cosyn Saunders'" suit, which seems to have been finally rejected after a year's courtship :

My best Ladie,

I received of late a letter from my best beloved cosyn having before wrytten unto him with as forcible reasonnes as I could, to persuade him to desist from his endles laberinth and fruitles love, the conclusion whereof since (for ought I did see) could be but repentance, the continuance would be but the redoubling of greife, and to his former affliction the addition of a treble weight. His answere was that my too deare love unto him had procured in mee more impatience then he could alow of. For so farre was he from repentance, as that he preferred the acquaintance and least favoure of so noble and worthy a Ladie before the enjoying of the greatest Ladie in the world. When I read this I could not but bothe laughe and sighe ; laugh to see what a creature love can make of a wise man ; and sighe to see that my best and most honored Ladie had rejected this constant and more worthie man to make hir housband then (I protest) I knowe living. Alas poore lover, alas neglected servant,

125   and

and woe unto all men that at their first entrance
into love esteeme women as Angels, but being over-
taken with the wandering of their owne affectiones
doe finde them in the end no better then merciless
Tyrannes. My Ladie, I see, is not become like
Pigmalion's Image, of a marble stone, a faire woman,
but of a faire woman is turned into a marble stone.
I can doe no more, I can say no more, but onely
this, that I am heavie, sad and wearie ; wearie of my
life, wearie of my selfe, and wearie of whatsoever
heretofore did most delight mee, but most wearie of
all in thinking of my dearest, and worthiest, unfortunate Ladie whose wittes are farthest from home,
when they should be readiest to doe hir the best
service.

I see by his wryting to your daughter, and both
wryting and sending to me, and not to you, that his
suite is growen desperate : and therefore remaines no
more of my parte but after making confession and
taking leave to leave to folowe these wan hopes any
longer.

My confession then (good Madame) is this, that
never since I first breathed ayre, either did I or doe
I honor or love any woman above your worthy selfe.
But in my love are, and ever shalbe three sundrie
sorted ranckes. The first is my naturall affection to
myne owne generation : the second my passion of
love to a woman, which is somewhat higher and

hotter :

hotter : the third the conjunction of my soule with the soule of another, which is the best and greatest, and this is and ever shalbe peculiare to your castaway, and to no other creature in the world. But yet if he had maried my deare Ladie, who hath the best parte of my harte, but least parte of my soule, then had my soule bene twined with both yours to make up Salomon's threefolded coard, that is so hardlie broken. But it must be as it may be, that can not be as I wishe it. My conceite of this triple love, of affection, passion & conjunction I discovered unto you long agoe in a letter wherein I wrytt (before you had ever seene my cosyn) that there had bene in my minde a duel betwixt love and honestie, yet honestie was and ever should be crowned with victorie, and the hottest love of myne towardes any woman when it came to feight with honestie, should have both his edge rebated and his poynt buttoned. So I sayed and so I wil say and thinke while I live, and am the better herein confirmed for that of late I have light upon Mr Spensers opinion so rightlie agreeing with that which nature had taught mee before, as the same might be thought to have bene drawne out of his discipline. And bicause I know how much you delight in all good learning, and in such honest verses, and to adde also some better tincture to my loath-to-departe, I wil set them downe as he wrytt them :

All

All naturall affection soone doth cesse
  And quenched is wth Cupides greater flame :
But faithfull freindship doth them both suppresse
  And them with mayspring discipline doth tame
  Through thoughtes aspiring to eternall fame.
For as the soule doth rule the earthly masse
  And all the service of the bodie frame :
So love of soule doth love of bodie passe
No less than perfect gold surmountes the meanest brasse.

So now (Madame) my soule I confess is his, so farre
as one mannes soule may be another's, and foloweth
after him to comforte his poore distressed and
unpitied soule : my heart is yours, my dead heart,
wrapped up in sorrowe, and buried in despaire, yet
good enough to offer for a present to hir, whose
harte is become so perseles and senseles as it hath
lost understanding.

And seeing you have forsaken him, you shall with
him also reject mee, who am whollie his for ever.
And first I wil charme myne eies, that hereafter they
never see you : myne understanding I wil so bewitche
with strange illusions and fantomes, as it shall ever
apprehend you as a spirite or a specter, newlie crept
out of a grave, and then with frighting I will run
from you as faste as my feete can beare mee ; my ever
dying harte I wil cleave in peeces with continuall
fretting to see hir an enemie to hir selfe who unto
mee is so much endeared.

And hereafter you shall not neede to reprove my

prayses

prayses of you, nor to enquire the reasonnes where-
fore I prayse you, for when you are commended by
others I wil be silent, and byte my tongue betweene
my teethe; and wil for ever hate all the virtues for
your sake, that have made their cabine in the hard
and senseles rocke of your harte.

And so fare you wel for ever my faire, deare, and
unfortunate Ladie; not more deare then faire, but
much more unfortunate then either faire or deare:
and farewel your prettie and worthy children with all
good blessinges from him that blesseth all: and farewel my good freindes, your honest and kinde house-
holde: farewel Arberie my owne hoped heaven upon
earthe, my now tormenting hell, and farewel with
thee whatsoever thou shroudest from winde and
wether; farewell my loath-to-departe and my selfe,
for wee two wil goe seeke strange coastes together.
And last of all farewel long letter, not too long
bicause thou art my last: and when thou art gone
from mee shew to my deare Ladie in what schoole
thou wert brought up by these last woardes, which
all theyr former fellowes caried with them.

> Your good Ld͡ᵐ most infinitelie bound
> and readie to be commaunded
> for ever
> FRANCIS BEAUMONT.

In the postscripts that follow he becomes a little less

lugubrious, and in the last of them again refers to his
"counsaylor," *i.e.*, Anne's sister Mary, who in the
meanwhile has (apparently) married her second husband,
John Lougher, or "Captain" Lougher, as Sir Peter
Leycester calls him :

> I received this weeke a letter from my Ladie Gray,
> wherein shee wrytt unto mee that shee did hope that
> hir suite for hir sister should have good success,
> because in such matters I was verie fortunate. Thus
> not onely faire Phillida but Philidaes faire sister also
> doth flowte mee. And since I am flowted of all, fare
> you wel all, for I am gone from you all for ever.
> The last yeare I sent to my little Ladie Emelie* a black
> cocke and much blacke fortune folowed : this yeare I
> send hir a whyte cocke to see if change of colour wil
> change fortune. I must entreat you when you see my
> counsaylor to commend my hartiest love unto hir and
> to tell hir that though shee be a maried wife, yet I wil
> take leave to love hir for ever while I carrie within
> mee a harte that can love. If hir housband wil give
> mee this libertie (which is in myne owne power to
>   take

---

* He probably means Lady Newdigate's eldest daughter Mary, then
about thirteen years old. The allusion is no doubt to the Lady
Emilie, the heroine of the "Knight's Tale" in Chaucer's "Canterbury Tales," beloved by Palamon and Arcite. Chaucer's poem has
been reproduced by Dryden under the title of "Palamon and
Arcite."

take my selfe) he shall love my wife (when I have hir)
as much as pleaseth him, and for his kindnes I wil
love him farre the better. Though I love not you,
yet for your sake I love all your generation.

This long and piteous letter seems to have worked upon
Lady Newdigate's feelings so far as to induce her to
seek a personal interview with the writer at Bedworth.
No sooner does she leave than he writes again what we
take to be the last letter of the series :

My best ladie,
Presentlie after your departure from Bedworthe, my
cosyn Saunders sent his footeman unto mee with a
letter, the coppie whereof I send you here inclosed.
It is beyond the limitation of my commission to
impart unto you his secret meaning unto mee : but
since everie freeman hath a wil, I wil also as wel as
others sometimes use my freedome.
I perceive playnlie this matter is growen to an end,
and that my long worke of subtraction hath bene but
a drawing of nothing out of nothing, whereof y^e
remaine is nothing, save nothing, after more then a
whole yeares wel-wishing unto you. If his most
affectionate love towardes you, and your kinde love
towardes him, and my bothe kinde and affectionate
love towardes you bothe must end but with a shorte
blacke crotchet, as Orlando di Lasso closed up (it
perisheth) when I have sayed but this (I am for ever

sorye)

sorye) then I have done. After many troubles y^t
have chaunced bothe to my cosyn and mee in prose-
cution of this desire, our hope was, that God would
in the end turne our mourninges to mirthe, unloose
our sackes, and girde us with gladnes, which had
come to pass if this had happened, and that our hope
of Cynthines conjunction had not proved a wry
aspect of a sextile.

What I could I have done and all that I have done
proceeded of a most sincere love unto you bothe.
Yet I must confess that in my laboures I did not a
little respect my selfe, when I thought, by enter-
course with two such excellent and worthy frendes,
that Arberie should have bene my little heaven upon
earthe, where all my misfortunes, my melancholie
passiones, and heapes of greife should have found
their present remedies. But like as Troylus once
sayed, so I say :

> All this I did, and I can doe no more ;
> She cruel is and woe is mee therefore.

This is the last time that ever I wil move you in this
or any matter to like purpose, taking my leave of
this suite as my cosyn hath done of Warwickshire in
his former letter unto mee. Yet never wil I forget
that I have obtained the frendshippe of a most noble
Ladie, which I ever hope to holde though my cosyn
have miste the accomplishment of his desired love.

And

And so wishing continuallie to possess the same by whatsoever service I can devise, I take my leave and rest

> Your good Lad⁻ most infinitelie
> bound and readie to be commaunded
>
> FRANCIS BEAUMONT.

My brother my sister my neece with all the best of this societie salute you in moe kind wordes then a sheete of paper can containe.

If it please you, the sworde may be sent by this bearer my cosyn Saunders boy.

The occasion of my cosyn Saunders letter unto mee whereof I have sent you the Coppie was this. Upon Mounday his man coming to Bedworthe with my Ladie Grayes letter I sent him all that night with a letter of myne to his master to have had him to have met you at Bedworthe upon Tewsday.

But you see his love is dying, not as vertuous soules departe in myldnes, or as men leave this world after a consumption, but with such desperate panges as are much more to be pitied by many degrees then I thinke they are. Of mee I knowe they are pitied even with my soule's greife: of you I knowe not how, you know best for I know nothing yᵗ lyeth hid in other hartes.

In this sad fashion exit "Cosyn Saunders" from the life-story of our heroines. We hear no more of him, but if

our

our supposition is right, and he was Matthew Saunders, of Shankton in Leicestershire, about this date he consoled himself by erecting an elaborate monument to the memory of his first wife, Margaret Skipwith, although her death took place in 1605, seven or eight years before his final dismissal as a wooer of Lady Newdigate. Neither has Anne preserved any later letters from Francis Beaumont. The latter may still have been a neighbour occasionally, although his brother and host, Sir Thomas Beaumont, died in 1612. It was five years later, in 1617, that Francis Beaumont was appointed (fourth) Master of the Charterhouse. He died in 1624, and is buried in the chapel. On his monument an effigy of him may be seen kneeling at a desk.

It may be interesting to students to know that he it was who, in 1597, addressed to "his very loving friend Mr Thomas Speght," a "judicious apology for the supposed levities of Chaucer" prefixed to the 1598 edition of Chaucer's works, and erroneously attributed to Francis Beaumont the poet (then only thirteen years old).

CHAPTER VII

The Valley of Death

ONE of Anne Newdigate's chief friends was Elizabeth, daughter of Edward Nevill, Lord Abergavenny, and wife of Sir John Grey, eldest son of Lord Grey of Groby. In Francis Beaumont's letters she is frequently mentioned as a friend and near neighbour in Leicestershire. There are a number of letters from Lady Grey to her "Deerst Sister" Anne Newdigate in the Muniment Room at Arbury, but are chiefly about her own concerns. She became a widow in October 1611, and then seems to have had some trouble with her father-in-law, Lord Grey of Groby, about money matters, her husband having died involved in debt.

Anne

Anne proved herself a sympathetic and useful ally in her friend's difficulties, and she has preserved the draft of a letter from herself to Lady Graye about this period which is so prettily expressed that it is given here as an example of her happier style :

My harts al honoring La : I did forbeare to send these wch misfortune cast into my custody till so fitt an opertunity gave me cause to present them on to you : These are al that came to my hands but only one deede wch my weake opinion tells me is as well with helde since as safe in my keepinge as my love to your worthy self is assured. Al the actions of my pore lives pilgermages performance (of use to you) is to solicite our merciful redimer to whom I daily offer my sincere prayers that he would be pleased to power uppon you as many blessed comforts as in his rich goodness he vouchsafeth to bestowe uppon his best beloved. W^th the presentation of my service to your deare selfe do humbly take my leave, And must cease to live before I can cease to be

faithfully yours
A. N.

Lady Grey's answer is as follows :

Deare Sister I have receaved by My worthy frinde Mr Sanders all those thinges which your love haith so carfully kepte for mee : for the deede you have

don

don mee a great favor to retaine it for it wolde be
dangrus for mee to have it till busnises are better
setled betweene my lord and my frinds for the good
of my childrin. I only desir a coppye of it by the
first opertunity that I may shewe it councell to knowe
of whatt strangth it will be to tye my lord Gray :
my ieys will not give me leve to say more of this or
of any other busnis so I leve it to this worthy berer
that shall truly make you know the state of all my
businese : and for all thos infinit favors which every
[h]our your love gives mee the best satisfacttion must
be my affecttion with infinit wishes for your hapines
which I can never exepres by my hand or any other
way: excepte your faithe wear as your most affectionat
sister sends them

E. GRAYE.

I send my most deerst love to my sweete goddaughter
with many good wishes for her happie fortune and the
like to the rest of your sweette childrin.

Lady Grey's affection for her friend prompted her to
write warmly in favour of an aspirer to Anne's hand
about this same date. No names are mentioned, but it
seems likely that the trusted "berer" in the last letter is
the "worthy frind" for whom she pleads :

My deerst sister If I had thought your lines wolde
have brought mee this hoples newes of my worthy
frinds affecttion I wolde have leffte to have chalinged

you

you for the necklect and have desired your lines of
another subiett, for I must confes you have handled
this so exslently as I knowe not howe to frame any
answer to chalinge anythinge you say, for I am in
that state you are in but much more unfortunat and
I coulde infinitly comend your resolution yf it were
any other that offered affecttion : but when I remember whom it is and whatt happines his worthynes
promisis I must needs tell you that your to infinit
care may take away that happines which myght give
much content both to you and yours. God knows
you are most deere to mee and so are your sweete
childrin in my best wishes and yf any thought did
tell my hart this match shoulde be the lest [w]ronge
to you or yours, yf it weare for my brother, my hand
shoulde never be so false to my hart as to solisit you
by my lines to tye you to the lest discontent : but it
is needles for mee to plede for him that can with the
life of true affection plede for him selfe and to him I
leve it with my deerst wishes all may be as happie to
you as to my live which is devoted to be everlast-
ingly

Your affectionat sister

E. GRAYE.

In spite of so many advocates for a second marriage, we
are glad to record Anne continued to " live maister of
herself," and remained Anne Newdigate to the end.

Lady

Lady Grey married again in 1614. Her second husband was a Mr. Bingley, afterwards Sir John Bingley. Her eldest son by Sir John Grey was created Earl of Stamford in 1628.

In this year, 1614, Anne's old friend Sir William Knollys, now Lord Knollys, was appointed Master of the Wards, and she had occasion to appeal to his jurisdiction in regard to pending suits concerning her son's property. Doubtless Anne thought (and rightly as it turned out) that in memory of past times the new Master of the Wards would give every attention to petitions emanating from his former " Gossepp."

Anne's copies of her petitions still exist in two well-thumbed papers in her own handwriting. They are quaintly worded, and are evidently her own composition :

Right hon^{ble} [she writes] haveing ever bin most bound to yor Los^p though never meriting anythinge, doe presume of the continueance of yor Losp: favoure to me & my Sonne being the Kinge's Ward, now under y^r honores jurisdiction, knowinge yor noble disposition to all & my selfe heretofore liberally tasting thereof, am thereby encouraged in this bold manner to be my Sonn's solicitore to yor Losp: himself being young, not able to be his own intercessor, Thoughe I hope & shalt thinke myself most happie if in time he may attaine to that perfection to be held

worthy

worthy to do yor Losp: any service. It hath pleased
God since Mr Newd: death (al noble Lord) that
sundry sutes & trobles have befallen me in respects
of my Sonns estate heare; being amongst a people
of strange dispositions, wch I thanke God by this
gentleman Mr Chamb: [Chamberlyn*] meanes have
well over passed, whoe is my near Neighboure and
most willing to Do me al freindly offices in my
rightful causes. . . . .

She then enters into particulars of her special grievances,
complaining

that it hath enforced me to call them in to the Court
of Wards and to have sutes (being a Woeman and
unfitt for these affaires) uppon process sent out of the
Court of Wards. 3 Tearmes since [they] have not
apeared all to procure mee more troble & charge
wch is ever incident to pore unfortunate Woemen in
my case. . . . . But since it hath pleased God to
place yor Losp: to be my Sonns judge I must confess
I shall wth much better comfort seek to defend his
right, although it hath ever bin my resolution since
it pleased God of his great mercy to bestowe the
wardship of my Child upon me, what in the power
of

* Probably the owner of Astley Castle of that name, and consequently a near neighbour, Astley Castle being only a mile and a
half from Arbury.

of my pore endeavoures lieth whereby to settle his estate quietly or keepe it as I found it that I may be blameles shall not be neglected, etc. etc.

This petition evidently met with a favourable response from Lord Knollys. A year later she frames another letter begging him to enforce the payment of the costs he had decreed should be paid her in this suit, which we hope was also successful.

Anne had other cares for her children at this time. She had not overlooked their future marriages, even when they were still in childhood. On more than one occasion she had some correspondence with friends as to an advantageous alliance for her boy. When he was only fourteen years old, she induced a friend, one Robert Phillips, to take a journey into Lincolnshire to make inquiries about a damsel but eleven years of age. Her name is not mentioned, but from the care with which she seems to have been guarded from the eyes of strangers, she must have been of special value as a matrimonial prize. " Pore Robin," as Mr. Phillips calls himself, seems to have fared somewhat badly on this quest :

Good Maddam [he writes] my long and unmannerly staye in yo' Ladishippe's house at my last beinge heare is the cause that pen and paper now present the tenour of my embassage in to Lyncollenshyre rather then my person. I have effected what you required, founde the gentell woman to be eleaven yeares old

and

and no more, neither yet fullye that—no speache of mariadge ether to your nevew or annye other in these partes. She is brought up in her father's house and a pretty gentlewoman as report goes. I sawe her not, but of this I am assured, I might with much more ease have seen all the monuments at Westminster, the lyons in the tower, jack napes and all the beares in parishe garden. Pore Robin was plundged in a cadge so deep that he had rather dive into fower and twenty suche cadges as once he was in then run into it agayne. And yet thanke God I am here ; but whilest I live I'll never run more there. God bless me from suche holes. I have a great busines for Thomas Beaumond wch I must needes effecte before I can see Arbery. I laye at his father in lawes at Lyncollen from the 10th daye till Shrove tuesday, and from that tyme at Coleorton till the mundaye after pallme sondaye, and God willinge, I will be with him agayne on wensdaye at nyghte, and there will lye the most parte of this somer and so soone (as possibly I can) I will attend your ladishippe's service (till when) I am ever comendynge yor ladyshippe and al yor prittye checkynges to heaven's protection ; not omitting my pritty megge wth her two sharpe teethe and all the rest in generall : Sente from Aldridge this present St George his daye, and remayne your Ladishippe's ever whilest he is his owne to comande

ROBERT PHILLIPS.

When

When I am married forsoothe, then I am at my
wyffe's comandes.

But Anne was not destined to live to see her beloved
Jack prosperously married, nor even to be released from
her anxious wardship.

In the autumn of 1617 she writes to her faithful
steward, William Henshawe, who was doing business
for her in London, addressing the letter as follows :

To my good servant Mr Willi: Henshawe at the Signe
of the Crowne neare St Martins Gate give these.

Good Willi :

Mr Holbitche can not pass without two or three
words, he can tell you of our health, al well I thank
God but my legg. I pray for yor busines and sone
returne. If Mr Thomson be at Whitehall goe see
him & Mr Leuston from me wth thanks for al
curtesies. I pray you enquire what becomes of Ned
Lume my old servant, for I fear Jo: will not be suffycient for the place. At my cousin George Crookes
you may heare of him, for he serves my Cousin
Boostred's eldest brother. Mr Holbitch is in great
hast, you may imagine so by my scribbling. Wth
al our remembrances to your good selfe do leave you
to God being ever

       Your old M^{ris} assured

         A. NEWDIGATE.

Arbery, Oct. 27, 1617.

A month

A month later she writes again :

Good Willi :

You have spent a great time in Atendance & never the better, only I can not but beleive there sloweness shewes the poreness of their title.   I desire peace if it may be, & so I pray you tell Mr Reede, & commend my love to him & Mr Verney ; but if it can not be to Jacke, it shall not be to me.

I was so ill uppon thursday that I could not write to you & am not much better at this time, my legg much trobleing me, althoughe little paine.   It is to no pur-poss to troble Mr Mathias about it, Unless he sawe the manner of it, for I dare applye nothinge unless I had his presence.   Mr Mountfort is very carefull, butt knowes nott what to make of it.   God's holy wil be done. . . .

Excuse me to al my freinds that at this time I write not to, for I can ill endure to sitt long.   Also my eyes are not well able to endure to write. . . .

Am now offerred a match for one of my Daughters, one Mr Kireton.   I bade yor uncle write to you to enquire of Mr Willi : Wright, but Jacke must leade the way.   I sent you a note of spice & other thinges. I feare yor purse will scarce hold out.   If not, I must supply it ; but I thinke new fruits will not come in till very neare Christmas, & I neede not any thinge that I have sent for, but a little before the time.   I

thinke

thinke Bousworth the carrier of Nuneaton goeth one jorney more before Christmas. You may enquire of him being now in London, he carryes for three farthinges the pound wch is cheaper then any other.

I pray you gett raphe Hayward to buy for me tow such lanthornes as he bought for me to stick on a wall. Comend me to yor sister & tell hir that the lace I gave hir for Jackes ruffe was butt 15 yeards; if it be not enoughe as I thinke it is not, lett me knowe what wanteth, & I will send it, for there was 3 yeards left behinde.

She then sends excuses to various friends for not answering their letters:

It is my unaptness that hinders. I hope you wil not be long from home, God send us a comfortable meeteing, al my deare children are well I humbly thanke God & comend their loves to you. . . . I pray you comend me to M^ris Gresley & thanke her for hir care; intreate that hir Lady may not knowe of the safphir by any meanes, I would have just such A one as that was hir Lady gave me or else none: I will cease yor troble and my owne & leave you to God's blessed keepeing being ever

Yo^r M^ris & freind ever assured

A. NEWDIGATE.

I have writt to Sr Franc. Englefield to enquire out a

match for Jack ; put him in minde thereof &
entreate my servante Bossone to do as much.

Excuse me to my cosin Ned Fitton. I was about to
write to him & Mr Chamb : came & stayed as long
as he could see. By my cousin Boustreds horses
uppon thursday I wil write if please God. If you
can learne the time of any of my friends purposs of
being here before you come, I pray you send
wordte.

My clock I feare is quite spoiled ; it gett 2 howers in
12, & will strike but one in every hower.

There is one more letter written to W. Henshawe four
days later, in which she takes advantage of " my cousin
Boustred's horses goeing " to send the answers to those
" good friends " to whom she could not write before.

The tearme's end [she writes] I hope will send you to
us ; but if we agree not of peace I pray you knowe of
my Cosin Croke, whether in the vacation they can
not put A trick uppon us, in respect it is under A
colloure for the kinge. Dale gives great words ; so
doth Anthony Robinson, but I respect them as I do
the speakers. We are all well I humbly thanke God.
Only my selfe, & that the least matter ; my legg I
knowe not what to saye of it or do to it but God's
blessed wilbe done. I pray you lett Mr Mathias
knowe that I have drunke seurby grass this 6 weekes
both morninge & after noone & purposs so to do

still. I have noe more to troble you with al but to deliver the lace & rebine to yo' sister. Jack comends him unto you & bids you tell Willi: Butterton that the lampe had 3 holes in it. A tinker was faine to mend it; he must furnishe him wth some oile for it. We had from Coventrie & it is so vile that it smells al the house over. Farewell good Willi: comend my love to al my good friends wisheing you A happie jorney & good returne do comite you to God remaineing ever

     Yo' M^ris & assured

Nov^b the 26 friend

 1617   A. NEWDIGATE.

Comend me to Sr Walter Leueson & tell him I hope he will see Arbery in his returne. I heare Sr George Curson went to London this weeke; if he did I pray you tell him that I take it very unkindly that he would not see me; I hope he beleives that I would have bin most glad to have sene him at Arbery if he do not he doth me the more wrong tell his La: Daughter so.

These three letters must have been preserved as amongst the last Anne wrote, for early in the following summer (to use her own words) God called her. In the prime of life, being only forty-three years of age, she was taken away, leaving five children to lament the loss of a mother at a critical period of their young lives, the

147   eldest

eldest being just twenty and the youngest only eleven years old. Thus she never lived to see her anxious wardship brought to an end; the active brain ceased to work and the loving heart to beat on behalf of the children for whom alone she seemed to live.

In accordance with the directions in her will, she was taken to Harefield to be buried. If she had died at Gawsworth, her desire was to have been laid at rest in the home of her youth. But as she passed away at Arbury her remains now lie beside her husband in the old family burial-place of Harefield. There they rest within the walls of that quaint and picturesque old church, which stands in solitary beauty in an oasis of green meadow land, whilst behind it rises a noble background of fine old trees.

Anne's effigy on the sculptured monument to her husband's memory erected in her lifetime is not a flattering representation of her, and bears little resemblance to her portraits at Arbury, of which there are four.

The latest of these must have been executed about four years before her death. It is a full-length portrait, where she is depicted standing by a table with a fan in her hand. In spite of her large hoop she looks slight in figure, and her countenance is pale and wan. Her gown is of black velvet with a ruff closed at the throat, and the red embroidery of her high-heeled shoes gives the only touch of colour to her dress.

148   Her

Her will, a copy of which, entirely in her own handwriting, is at Arbury, is dated in 1610, the year of her widowhood. Much of the first part is copied from her husband's will, to which she was left sole executrix.

She begins, as was customary at that time, with a profession of her faith:

In the name of the father and of the sonne and of the holye ghost Amen.

I dame Anne Newdigate, late wife of S[r] John Newdigate Knighte, beinge in health of bodye and in perfect and good memorye thanks be to my mercifull God for the same, at the makinge of this my last Will and Testament w[ch] I ordaine etc. etc.

First I bequeath my soule into the hand of God my maker & creator and to Jesus Christ my blessed Savio[r] and Redimer, and to the Holye Ghoste my blessed sanctifier. . .

And I bequeath my bodie to the earth from whence it came, desiringe either to bee buried in Herfield churche by my husband, S[r] John Newdigate or in Gawesworth Churche by my deare ffather S[r] Edward ffitton w[th]out anie extraordinarye cost, but in a comelie manner, as is fitt, w[th] some small memorie of mee, as my name, and my husband and ffather's Armes together in some windowe sett. I desire to be buried at Herfield unlesse it shoulde please God I shall dye at Gawesworth since it is God's will that I should

149   outlive

outlive my husbande S^r Jo. Newdigate, and he makinge
mee his executrixe, leavinge mee in trust wth his
Children, and all that ever he had in the worlde, I
hereby charge my Executo^{rs}, as they answere before
God at the generall daie of Judgement, that whatsoever shalbe lefte unpformed of his my husband's
Will at my death, that it be truelie and faythfullie
performed. Item I give to my sonne Jo. Newdigate
all chattells, goods, plate, househould stuffe, stocks of
cattell quicke or deade that I shall have at the time of
my death remayning unbequeathed, my Will being
first performed, the remainder to my sonne Jo :

Lady Newdigate then wills certain portions to her
daughters and to her second son, who inherits some
land as well, and continues :

And whereas out of my deare love to my eldest
sonne and for the better upbuilding of his house,
I have hereby wholly given and disposed the profitt
of his wardshippe and marriage to those uses the
sooner to free his landes in Middlesex etc. . . yet
he shall pay each of his sisters Thirtye pounds apeece
yearly until they are married or their portions are
paid to them . . . . And I earnestlye desire and
charge William Whitall as he was left in trust by
his M^r my husband S^r Jo : Newdigate and nowe
by mee that my boyes may be brought uppe in
good learninge and both they and my daughters to

be

be bred uppe in virteous and godlie lyffe in our
Catholick and Protestant Religion to the under-
standinge of God's holie Will and wayes revealed in
his greate compassion and mercie unto us by his
divine Gospell and in the true faith of Jesus Christ
our onelie Savio' Redeemer and Mediator, whome I
beseache in his abundant mercie make them all five of
his chosen elect. And when my boyes are of fittynge
learninge and yeares that they maye goe to the Univer-
sities and Innes of Courte. And I charge William
Withall that my eldest sonne be not married before
hee be Sixteene yeares oulde at the least, and not then
nor ever against his owne Will and good likinge by
anie interest challenged over him by my righte. . . .

She then divides her "gownes, petticoats, jewells" and
other valuables amongst her five children. She bequeaths to Richard the bedstead with the yellow velvett
canopy and taffata quilt "wth my uncle Francis Fytton
gave me." To her mother, who survived her, she left
a ring which her father had given her:

Item my Will and desire is to have a fewe playne
gould Rings made of tenne or twelve shillinges price
wth a pansie being my ffather's Crest, engraven on
the outside and two letters for my name enamelled
wth blacke on either side the pansie and an inscription w^thin to be in lattyn, these wordes followinge:
Death is the begininge of life; and to be delivered

unto

unto soe manie of my friends as a memorie of my love as I heare nominate :

Amongst those she here mentions is her sister, Mary Polwhele, the date of this portion of her will being shortly after William Polwhele's death and before the Lougher marriage.

The last part was added in 1615, when she goes on :

I nowe make and ordaine my ho^ble kinsman Sr Francis Englefield Knighte Baronett, William Whitall and William Henshawe my two servants, my three Executo^rs. I did [not] nominate S^r ffrancis till I had spoken wth him who hath promised me to take care of my Children. . . .

In witnesse that this is my Will and Deede I sette my hande the ffower and twentieth of October in the yeare of O^r Lorde 1615.

ANNE NEWDIGATE.

We know no more of the last days of Anne, Lady Newdigate. Her mother and her sister may have been with her at the end, for they both survived her by many years.

On one side of the elaborate monument erected to her father, Sir Edward Fytton, in Gawsworth Church, is the seated figure of his widow, Lady Fytton, her head resting on her hand. Behind her appear her two daughters, Anne and Mary, kneeling, whilst her two sons are in a like attitude in front.

Of Mary Lougher we can ascertain only that she was again left a widow in 1636, when she took out letters of administration to her second husband's estate. We are indebted to Mr. Bridgeman for this information and also for the discovery of her will. Had it not been for his unwearied and persistent efforts, we should be without the glimmer of light afforded us by these wills of Polwhele and Mary, and the administration to Lougher. We desire again to record our gratitude to him for the time and pains he has expended in procuring valuable information, and also for his useful criticism of the manuscript of this work.

Mary Lougher's will is dated December 19, 1640, and was proved in the Prerogative Court of the Archbishop of Canterbury on July 5, 1647: it was proved a second time, before the Probate Court established by Cromwell, on September 22, 1653. The executors appointed by the will were her son, William Polwhele, and her daughter, Elizabeth Lougher, but probate was granted to William Polwhele alone, as "surviving executor."

She bequeaths the lease of Perton to her son, William Polwhele; the lease of Rinkeston or Rinteston and Killkelly in Pembrokeshire to her daughter, Elizabeth Lougher. She makes bequests to her "little grandchild Ann Gattachree," to her son-in-law, John Gattachree, his wife and three children. She mentions her

son-in-law,

son-in-law, Robert Chernnock, and gives directions for
her burial at Goulsworth (Gawsworth), Co. Chester.

Thus she apparently continued to flourish like a green
bay-tree until 1647, the date of her death, when she
must have been sixty-nine years old.

In bidding farewell to Mary Fytton, with all the
difficulties that obscure her career, we cannot but hope
and believe that the brilliant maid of honour, frail
though she undoubtedly was, had qualities of heart and
soul to enable her to benefit by the love and example
of her faithful sister. And as Anne was charitable to
her failings to the last, so may we also be.

It may be interesting to jot down here as briefly as
possible the main facts in the after life of Anne's five
children.

Her eldest son, the much-loved Jack, married early
Susanna, daughter of Arnold Luls, a Dutch merchant
in London. They had one son, who died in infancy,
and when about his mother's age John died himself in
the year 1642.

The property then passed to his only brother Richard,
a lawyer of great ability and independent honesty. He
is known to history in Cromwell's time for having
refused to condemn the Earls of Bellasis and Dumfries,
with Colonel Halsey and other Royalists who were
tried before him at the York Assizes for levying war
against the Protector. Judge Newdigate observed that
"although by 25 Ed. III. it was high treason to levy

war

war against the king, he knew of no statute to extend
this to a Lord Protector." In consequence of this
independence of action he was deprived of his place,
but later restored to the Bench by the Commonwealth
after the Protectorate was abolished. Later on he was
made a baronet by Charles II. He married Julian,
daughter of Sir Francis Leigh of Newnham Regis, and
had a large family, from one of whom the present family
are directly descended, although the male line with the
baronetcy became extinct at the beginning of the present
century.

Of Anne Newdigate's daughters, the eldest, Mary, nick-
named " Waspsnest " by Sir Richard Leveson, married
Edmund Bolton of Granborough, Co. Warwick, but
none of her descendants survive, the last of them,
a daughter Lettice, having died unmarried in 1693-4.
Lettice Bolton was buried in Astley Church, where it
is recorded on her monument that she " lived very
hansomly upon a narrow fortune ; her life was without
trouble, and her death without pain."

Anne's second daughter, Lettice Newdigate, died
unmarried at the age of twenty.

Anne, the youngest, who was only eleven years old at
the time of her mother's death, married Sir Richard
Skeffington, Kt., second son of Sir William Skeffington,
Bart., of Fisherwick, Co. Stafford, and their son, who
married the daughter of Sir John Clotworthy, 1st
Viscount Massarene, succeeded to that peerage under

155   the

the special remainder of the patent on the death of his father-in-law. Lady Skeffington died when only twenty-nine, and an admiring friend (possibly the "Cousin Boustred" of Lady Newdigate's letters) has perpetuated her memory in a monument erected by him in St. Michael's Church, Coventry. The inscription is as follows :

An Elegicall epitaph made upon the death of that mirror of women Ann Newdigate, Lady Skeffington, wife of that true moaneing turtle Sir Richard Skeffington, Kt., & consecrated to her eternal memorie by the unfeigned lover of her vertues, Willm. Bulstrode, Knight.

> Vertue humble, beautie chaste, pious wit,
> Husband's honour, women's glorye, sweetlye knit,
> And all comprised fairelye in this one,
> Sad fate hath here enshrined with this stone.
> Vertue triumph, for thou hast woon the prize ;
> Beautie teach women to be chast & wise ;
> Make her your patterne of a vertuous life
> Who lived & died a faire unspotted wife.
> She was the mirror of her age and dayes
> And now the subject of transcendent prayse.
> O what a harmonye man's life would be,
> Were women all but neare as good as she.

> • • • • •

Obiit Maii 21 ætatis suæ, 29 anno Dni 1637.

Our

The Valley of Death

Our self-imposed task is at an end. Farewell Anne, Dame Newdigate, true daughter, sister, wife and mother. We trust we have done you justice. It has not been for lack of love and admiration if we have failed.

For us, living as we do within the same walls where nearly three hundred years ago, Anne lived, loved and died, where her portraits look down upon us from dining-hall and gallery, our chief heroine's personality has a reality and a fascination which we cannot hope to impart to our readers.

We would, however, hope that Anne's true womanly life may still have an influence for good on the posterity she longed to benefit. May we one and all so learn the true lesson of this life's pilgrimage as to be able to echo from our hearts the last message to her friends of the first Lady Newdigate of Arbury :

" Death is the begiñinge of life."

APPENDIX

Extracts from a list of Anne Newdigate's expenses, showing that she was evidently a visitor to Mary Polwhele at Perton in 1607

Item chickens 14.	. . . . .	.	0	2	4
It : 6 chickens	. . . . .	.	0	1	2
It : clarett wine	. . . . .	.	0	2	0
It : a dozen & halfe of pigeons	. . .	.	0	2	3
It : for rosmarye flowers	. . .	.	0	0	4
It : halfe an elle of lace for lettice	. . .	.	0	2	0
It : to Mr Mathyas	. . . .	.	0	10	0
It : broumes	. . . . .	.	0	0	4
It : to goodwife gardener for her halfe yeare's wages ending at 1607 ou^r La : daye	. .	.	0	15	0
It : 12 ducklings	. . . .	.	0	2	6
It : aquavita	. . . . .	.	0	1	6
It : 5 couple of rabets	. . .	.	0	3	0
It : to Will : Walker the Joyner	. .	.	0	0	9
It : tow pans more then the ould	. .	.	0	5	1
It : Wooden ware for the dogs house	. .	.	0	1	0

159   Item a pore

Appendix

	£	s	d
Item a pore man	0	0	4
It : a girdle for dicke	0	2	6
It : peirceing 50 pearls	0	1	6
It : makeing Malls ringe	0	1	0
It : a paire of shooes for Jacke . . .	0	1	0
virginall wiers	0	0	4
It : a paire of shoes for myself . . .	0	2	6
It : a paire for lettice	0	1	0
It : the shoemaker's man	0	0	4
12 elles of cloeth weaving & tow dossen of napkins	0	1	0
It : nursse on her goeinge	0	10	0
It : 12 yeards of cobbweb lawn . . .	0	8	0
It : 6 threed laceses	0	0	6

At my being at perton

	£	s	d
It : the keeper at Brude parke . . .	0	10	0
It : the keeper's men	0	2	0
It : in the house at perton . . .	0	8	0
It : to my sister for silver chamlett . .	1	0	0
It : Docter Cherriboode	2	0	0
It : at Sʳ Walter Leueson	0	4	6
It : mending the Coatch	0	2	6
It : my sisters nursse	0	2	0
etc. etc.			

Printed by BALLANTYNE, HANSON & Co.
London & Edinburgh

Printed in the United States
88703LV00007B/224/A

9 781432 686390